Praise for *The Inward Outlook*

"*The Inward Outlook* is the most direct read I've come across that gets to the nuts and bolts of how to live a more authentic and productive life. We humans like to complicate things, and Dr. Basha brings the reader back to where the problem and the solution live, which is within us. She explains the inward outlook paradigm, and shows the reader how to take simple steps to make it work in their lives. For a person ready to become more conscious, grounded, and authentic, *The Inward Outlook* simplifies the path to living a life of purpose through conscious choices."
—RACHAEL WOLFF, podcaster and author
of *Letters from a Better Me*

"How refreshing to read *The Inward Outlook* and be reminded that how we think affects who we are and how we are in the world. I'm grateful for Dr. Laura Basha's teachings, which offer a path toward living a more joyful, peaceful, and authentic life through finding and expressing our truest self."
—JUDY REEVES, author of *Wild Women, Wild Voices* and
A Writer's Book of Days

"Dr. Laura Basha has an indelible charisma and a personal presence in her writing and delivery. Within what may be intellectually familiar themes of *The Inward Outlook*, I found as I read—as you may—that I actually experienced the meanings of these themes bringing forward from past thoughts and memories, new connections to my own complex, present-day perception of reality. "
—MARGARET BARBEE, PhD, Senior Human Resources
Consultant, former professor, and Director of
Organizational Psychology Programs at JFK University

"As we navigate these troubled and remarkable times, *The Inward Outlook* offers a perspective that guides people in the awakening of personal consciousness with a compassionate lightheartedness. Bringing decades of study and experience to her work, Dr. Basha articulates the essential importance of developing an inner awareness to the struggles of daily life and speaks to the transformation that can emerge by opening to the possibilities of growth and happiness within. Awakening to the self takes focus, and the included workbook provides the reader with a structure to discover who they are and who they want to be."
—CHERYL KRAUTER, MFT, author of *Odyssey of Ashes: A Memoir of Love, Loss, and Letting Go* and *Surviving the Storm*

"*The Inward Outlook* gently reawakened me to several simple and accessible actions to take to have more joy, happiness, and peace in life. This work is phenomenally empowering."
—XAVIER DUBOIS, CEO of EVOX Omnimedia

"After ninety-one years of an intensive quest to find the causes of human suffering, to reduce or alleviate it, I can summarize my conclusion in one sentence: There can be no freedom possible unless each one of us is free from ourself. Dr. Basha presents one path toward that freedom. Through understanding *The Inward Outlook* paradigm, we can change the acculturated reality of ourselves by accessing an internal space of Silence and letting eternal wisdom flow through us. We can develop a perceptual shift and learn to make conscious choices to create a life of fulfillment and peace of mind."
—R.K. JANMEJA (MEJI) SINGH, PHD, author of *Changing the Course of Destruction: Listening to Understand Each Other In-Depth Promotes Peace* and recipient of the California State Psychological Association's Lifetime Achievement Award

"Learning to live more deeply in the present is a powerful tool for personal growth. This cultivates a deeper self-awareness that allows us to question the perceptions that shape our sense of ourselves and our lives. By untangling unhelpful and inaccurate self-perceptions, our authentic selves are allowed to shine through. *The Inward Outlook* is a great place to begin cultivating this awareness of the self in the present moment."

—SHANNON DUNCAN, author of *Present Moment Awareness* and *Coming Full Circle*

"Dr. Laura Basha offers us a witty, contemplative way to evaluate and understand our lives in all their messy, contradictory, and inspiring pathways. With her common-sense framework for moving forward in life—a positive, lasting, and holistic approach—we can indeed transform our thoughts and actions. Her book includes a reflective, hands-on study guide to help us see our lives in a new light, one that promotes self-awareness and a greater acceptance of our fellow beings."

—RICHARD SINGER, educator, author, and community activist

"Basha reminds us here of the importance of listening to the power of wisdom and grace innate in us all. With gentle humor and compassion, she brings forth a lightness and a possible way of creating a just world."

—REENIE RASCHKE, author of *My Town Montclair*

"*The Inward Outlook* reminds us that our ever-present center is challenged by the fast-paced, technically minded world we live in. With insight and down-to-earth humor, Dr. Basha helps us to find our awareness again."

—MONA ADISA BROOKS, professional artist and founder of Trumpet Gallery

"As a CEO and personally, I found the insights and lessons developed in *The Inward Outlook* to be profoundly impactful. The principles explained by Dr. Laura Basha will help anyone to be a more effective leader and better parent and spouse while at the same time growing and deepening their own understanding of their human experience. I utilize the principles she describes in the book to great success, and since embracing this understanding of life I've been able to put them to work and triple the size of our company. I would encourage everyone to explore the principles for themselves; the benefits will be profound."

—JIM HART, CEO of Senn Delaney Leadership
Consulting, a Heidrick & Struggles Company

"I have been studying and teaching various aspects of healthy functioning for individuals, teams, and organizations for over twenty-seven years, and I found *The Inward Outlook* to be one of the best, most thoughtful approaches I've encountered. Dr. Basha's clear and simple-yet-profound message resonates with our innate health and wisdom. I am blessed to know Laura personally, and know that she truly lives what she teaches. As a result, her sincerity and practical application come through in every facet of this wonderful book."

—JOHN MCKAY, Senior Vice President of
Senn Delaney Leadership Consulting,
a Heidrick & Struggles Company

THE
INWARD
OUTLOOK

Published 2023
Printed in the United States of America
Print ISBN: 978-1-64742-473-2
E-ISBN: 978-1-64742-474-9
Library of Congress Control Number: 2022912646

For information, address:
She Writes Press
1569 Solano Ave #546
Berkeley, CA 94707

Interior design by Tabitha Lahr

She Writes Press is a division of SparkPoint Studio, LLC.

THE
INWARD
OUTLOOK

Conscious Choice as a Daily Practice

LAURA BASHA, PhD

SHE WRITES PRESS

The Fool knows that she doesn't know anything.
Therefore she doesn't listen to what she knows,
She listens for what she doesn't know,
And thus becomes the wisest of all.

—LAURA BASHA

TO THE REVEREND KATHRYN JARVIS

*Whose illumined consciousness led us to the gates
of the Temple and showed us how to walk in alone.*

AND TO YOU, THE READER

May you be freed from the limitations of the past.

The Inward Outlook

The Inward Outlook distinguishes
a way of being in the world.

✳ ✳ ✳

This way of being radiates a lighthearted, wise,
and pragmatic perspective drawn from a deep understanding
of how thought creates each person's reality.

✳ ✳ ✳

The Inward Outlook is one articulation
of the Art of Transformation.

✳ ✳ ✳

*"There is no doubt that everyone
has the capacity to be happy.
Their happiness depends on their thoughts,
and everyone is capable of realizing the
power of their own thinking."*
—SYDNEY BANKS

Contents

Origin Story

Who knew a penniless, shy, anxiety-riddled
kid from the Boston suburbs would create
a lucrative global career teaching access to
beauty and peace of mind to thousands?

I HAD NIGHTMARES EVERY NIGHT OF MY LIFE until I was thirty-five. No kidding. Every night. That's what sleep was for me.

Ours was a childhood with no safe harbor and we grew up poor. My sisters and I were terrified of the unpredictable outbursts of both our parents. I figured out how to read the psychological undercurrents so as to stay out of their way by the time I was around eight years old. This essentially meant I became mute—did not share my thoughts or self-expression for fear of ridicule and punishment. Loneliness was a familiar companion. I found solace in drawing and painting, a form of expression that I have refined over the years and practice to this day.

I was ashamed of what I perceived as my family's inadequacies. Our rundown house sat in the midst of a well-to-do middleclass neighborhood of new 1950s homes. We had no front steps to the front door and the wooden porch on the side of the house was rotting and unpainted. The neighbors made fun of my dark-skinned, introverted father behind his back as he walked home from the bus stop after a long day working on the fishing docks of Boston, head hung low.

We did have a television, however, and I had a deep fascination with two TV programs: *One Step Beyond* and *The Twilight Zone*. I would finish my homework early on the afternoons they aired so that I made sure I could watch those weird and fascinating shows. There was something about other realms of existence that I think triggered an intrinsic awareness in me that the physical world was not the only option for information—that maybe I was more than this lost, anxious little girl.

As lowly as our circumstances were, I decided that I must not be worth much—but I wanted to feel safe, to be free of these past emotional patterns and ways of thinking about myself. I wanted to know how to access mental and emotional health and well-being. I kept searching for how to belong, how to harness true power and generate authentic self-expression. I had a longing for the dissolution of the illusion of separateness—to achieve oneness. I had a tremendous longing for peace of mind.

These longings brought me to California from the East Coast. My soon-to-be husband Bert and I drove out in our old Ford Falcon station wagon, and found housing and work in our new town of Oakland, CA. Searching for peace of mind didn't end, and through securing work as a color artist with a color and fashion studio, I met a coterie of people who were to become my new family, a tight circle of folks whom I still call friends. It was through this circle that I was introduced to the emerging transformational growth and development work that permeated the Bay Area in the '70s and '80s, and began to understand how to become free from the old limitations of childhood that had so repressed me—how freedom from the past could be available to anyone who was interested.

At the age of twenty-seven I met my spiritual teacher, the Reverend Kathryn Jarvis. Over the next seventeen years, she taught me and other students how to heal ourselves and others. We worked with requests for healing from people all over the world, and we received report after report stating, "The doctors were amazed!" as terminal illnesses like stage four cancer and HIV/AIDS cases disappeared from patients' bodies. What was not understood medically did not interfere with the truth of transmutation. I began to see how I could be an instrument of and catalyst for transformation and healing, and how healing old emotional wounds gave me access to being of service to others in the same way. "To give is to receive" suddenly made sense. It had to come through me first, then flow out to others.

Even with all this growth, I was still having nightmares, so when at the age of thirty-five I heard about a wonderful homeopath who worked at the Hahnemann Clinic on San Pablo Avenue in North Berkeley, CA, I went to see her. After several pages' worth of very odd questions (*Do you leave one foot hanging outside the sheets when you sleep at night? If so, which foot on which side of the bed?*), she prescribed a homeopathic remedy for me and . . . the nightmares stopped! Just like that. I was amazed, relieved—dumbfounded.

And thus I began to search in earnest about how to heal conditions, mindsets, hidden scars. I was still very much devoted to my work with the Reverend Jarvis; but I also wondered, *What other healing methodologies, solutions, and interventions might be sourced from outside of what can be seen or scientifically proven?*

During this time, I came across an ontological study that incorporated all levels of human psychological evolution, as well as all levels of spiritual evolution that can be experienced—eventually returning us to the Tao, which of course can only be pointed to. This study was an enlightened, pragmatic, and accessible version of those old metaphysical TV shows of the '50s and '60s. I was so influenced by it that I began to work with it intensively—and have continued to do so for the last nearly forty years.

I then met an exceptional man named Sydney Banks. He'd had an experience of theophany, a transmutational awakening experience with Light, years earlier, and since then people had been flocking to him and asking him to explain spirituality to them. Syd had inspired two very perceptive psychologists to work with him, and together they were pulling the worlds of spirituality and psychology together.

It was at this juncture that I went back to graduate school, first completing a master's program in counseling psychology and continuing on to get a double doctorate in clinical and organizational psychology. The two psychologists who had been working with Syd became mentors for me, and the model they developed with Syd became the model of psychology about which I wrote my dissertation and upon which I based my psychological practice.

Through these many years, I experienced divorce and became a single mom of two with no child support; completed graduate school; and weathered the devastating impact of my children's father's suicide. It was with the guidance of these above-mentioned extraordinary healers and mentors that I turned inward and was able—through the illuminating fires of self-reflection, understanding forgiveness, and ongoing personal transformational development—to release myself from the traumatic and invalidating mindsets within which I had been imprisoned. I found my way from crucifixion to resurrection.

When my father was ninety-one, I flew with my sister Betty from the SF Bay Area to his home in Portland, Oregon, after not having seen him for more than twenty years. My sister and I aligned on creating a mindset of love and affinity to bring to him for this visit. Through that alignment, I was able to tell this now fragile old man who had been the terror of my childhood that I loved him. With an impossibly remorseful and heartbreaking expression on his face he said back, "I love you too, honey." Compassion welled up within me, and over the following weeks we shared several tender phone conversations. He passed away six months later, on Father's Day. At the age of fifty-eight, I could no longer say I didn't know a father's love.

A few years later, my three sisters and I flew to New Hampshire to see my ninety-year-old mother. She had been truly neglectful to all of us in childhood—and yet I could honestly, authentically, and with gratitude say to her, "Mom, I love you, and I want to thank you for my life. You did your job, because I have a great life." She welled up with tears and we hugged. She made her transition seven weeks later.

These were not idle, contrived communications. These conversations with both my parents were heartfelt and powerfully transformative—and it took me decades of personal development to be capable of accessing the unflappable truth of love that I communicated to them both. The only realm that is real is love. This is no pollyannaish drivel. Accessing love in the face of trauma and fear is the way out of hell.

We are all on a learning odyssey through seemingly endless cycles of reincarnation. My life continues to be about this work. I know now how to walk through the fires and rise from the ashes—not untouched, but unscathed. My commitment is to share what I have learned and practiced and honed through the crucibles of my own experiences, so that others may find freedom from the limitations of the past, know how to access peace of mind, and live contented and creative lives.

Being free from the past allows you to non-judgmentally recognize the limitations of your old thought patterns so you can awaken to conscious choice and authentically and powerfully choose, express, and create in the present. Through cultivating an inward outlook, you will be able to realize a simple shift in thinking that loosens the grip of old, limiting thought patterns and brings an ongoing availability to wisdom, common sense, clarity, light-heartedness, and well-being—no particular sets of practices or exercises required.

Imagine a life filled with ease, authentic self-expression, and joy. Creativity, true power, and peace of mind emerge for you and become ever available as you awaken to masterful living. I share this work with love in the spirit and hope that some phrase or inquiry will inspire possibility in you, holding a mirror up to your own innate beauty, genius, and greatness.

—Laura Basha
Santa Rosa, California
November, 2022

PREFACE

THE INWARD OUTLOOK IS AN EXTENSION of my coaching and teaching work with people of all ages and walks of life. This revised version, coupled with the new addition of the Practices Book section, is intended to make the heart of the work available to a wider audience.

Developed, validated, and deepened over the last forty-plus years, this paradigm has proven its effectiveness not only in my life but in the life experience of the thousands of clients with whom I have worked. Intrinsic in the words of this book is the experience of my years in the fields of personal and organizational transformation, spirituality, creativity, and psychology.

In 1978, I met the Reverend Kathryn Jarvis—a woman who had the most significant influence on altering my perceptions about life. We called her Mrs. Jarvis—which, being a refined Southern woman, was her preference. She had been the head of the Unity Village training school and was the head of Silent Unity, the international prayer ministry of Unity Village in Missouri.

Kathryn Jarvis was a truly illumined soul. It was my great privilege to have fourteen years of training with her in the art of healing, spiritual principles, and the healing power of thought. She taught us not only through her words but, more powerfully, through her way of being. She taught us how to truly be in the moment, or as she said, how to "practice the Presence," and how all healing first takes place in the Silence. I am eternally grateful for my time with her, as Mrs. Jarvis reawakened my own self-realization.

It was in 1989 that I first heard the name of Sydney Banks. At that time, a good friend of mine was sharing her experience of transformational work through the teachings of an unusual man from Scotland. Though having only a grammar school education, Mr. Banks had had a spiritual awakening that transformed him from a shy and somewhat disgruntled man into a profoundly confident, secure, serene, and focused human being who became comfortable speaking to large audiences of highly educated people.

After having spent fourteen years studying the spiritual principles underlying healing work with Mrs. Jarvis, I continued on to study for the ministry. This study was followed by several years participating in the human-potential movement, at which point I became very intrigued by Mr. Banks.

Although my undergraduate work began in 1969 in the field of psychology, I became disillusioned with the academic approach to the field and switched my major to fine arts. Ideally, I wanted psychology to coalesce with grounded spirituality, but this combination was not available to me at that time. When I listened to my friend speak about this new work of Sydney Banks, however, something drew me to listen more deeply.

Within a year, I found myself attending a speaking engagement in 1990 at Mills College in Oakland, California, which was featuring Mr. Banks. He was co-leading a presentation on what he called the three principles of Mind, Consciousness, and Thought. Thus began the work that would become foundational in my clinical and coaching profession, for in this model was the integration of psychology and spirituality that I had been seeking to combine and study in the late sixties.

There is absolute simplicity inherent in *The Inward Outlook*, as its principles reveal the complexity of our habitual and familiar ways of thinking and functioning. Recognizing the complexity of our habitual thinking allows us to make changes toward simplicity, thus actualizing the qualities and choices of who we dream ourselves to be.

The simple shift of being able to distinguish between two possible ways of thinking that are intrinsic to all human beings fosters conscious choice. This is empowering. Conscious choice implies connection to our essence, to being present in the moment, where life actually and only occurs. Not only does this knowledge aid in discovering our true self-expression, it automatically moves us toward the full optimization of it.

Self-actualization then becomes simple and accessible, though not always easy. Taking the time to observe and identify your repetitive thought patterns becomes a way of living and allows for the emergence of your eternal essence, of who you are as timeless being. At first it's challenging, but eventually, with practice, it provides you with an overall sense of calm awareness coupled with a newfound lightness of spirit.

We come to realize that, indeed, we are all doing the best we can given the way we see life, and none of the inharmonious ways in which we operate or express need to be taken personally. What someone says simply reveals the way they see life at that particular moment.

These principles are shared in a pragmatic and digestible manner with the intention that you, the reader, may extract tools that will guide you to become more of who you've always known yourself to be: creative, inspired, compassionate, and effective. We can then *bring* to any circumstance, condition, or relationship whatever it is that we were hoping to *find*. We bring what we are looking for.

Instead of taking your cues from thoughts about external circumstances, you can take your cues from your own inner wisdom and common sense, resulting in a life experience of grace, ease, power, and authenticity.

INTRODUCTION

IS THERE ANY AREA IN YOUR LIFE IN WHICH you would like to move forward, or any area in which you feel entangled and would like to experience freedom? Are you dealing with any circumstance that feels so serious it often seems hopeless?

If you could experience insight and relief in one or all of these areas, would you be interested? Would you be interested if you could see any particular issue more lightly, and even grasp compassionate humor in the midst of great challenge? What if you could even have an epiphany of perfect clarity about it, or view the issue as an ideal setup to receive exactly what you want, would this be of value to you?

You can have such an experience. You can come away from reading this book with a shift in perspective that genuinely recognizes—in spite of appearances to the contrary—the possibility of hope for the probability of transformation.

How do we catalyze insightful perspective within ourselves, or in another person, rather than simply develop skill sets? Insightful perspective is available at any given moment, without the need for remembering particular studies, techniques, or mantras.

Transformation takes place when we have the experience of a perceptual shift that transcends memory. This is the perceptual vantage point of wisdom, insight, and lightheartedness. This perceptual shift arises from the state of being present and aware of your personal thought process and is the perspective of what I am calling "transformational humor."

Transformational humor emerges from understanding the interrelationship of the principles underlying *The Inward Outlook*. We will examine this quality of humor in depth, as it is an attribute of living from an inward outlook.

This transformational quality of humor is compassionate and allows us to view life from a neutral stance of alignment with our true personality and our innate authenticity. We then perceive circumstances and conditions from a larger order—a "bigger picture," if you will—than what was previously entertained.

One of the great benefits of understanding how to live from an inward outlook is the resulting ability to establish rapport between people in pretty much any circumstance. There is a thread of commonality that runs through all of us, in spite of culture, gender, or generation. This common unifying thread transcends the details and content of any situation. Cultivating an inward outlook reveals the commonality of our humanity.

Finally, *The Inward Outlook* is a principle-based framework that offers us better understanding of day-to-day life experience and what it means to be human. We will explore the positive shifts that awaken each of us to become healthy, creative, joyful, and authentic human beings. We will recognize our innate and profound capacities for compassionate wisdom, resilience, and insight while fostering lightheartedness and well-being.

NOTE TO READER

THERE ARE CERTAIN WORDS IN THE TEXT that I have intentionally capitalized. I have distinguished these words in this way as the capitalization points toward them being expressions of what we might call "Divine Attributes."

"Divine Attributes" refer to those qualities of Mind, or Source, that we aspire to inculcate, embody, and express as our own personal characteristics. These are attributes that we can intentionally cultivate having access to, in order to bring deeper understanding, compassion, and wisdom to our worlds and ourselves.

Capitalizing "Compassion," for example, distinguishes Compassion as an infinite and eternal realm, available to each of us through thought, as distinct from our own individual capacity to express the quality of compassion. Accessing one Divine Attribute actually gives access to all Divine Attributes. Compassion as a realm expands into Beauty as a realm, which expands into Love as a realm, and so forth, much as the colors of a rainbow blend into each other when sunlight is distinguished through a prism.

Capitalizing "Thought" refers to Thought as the realm of all possible Thought, the realm of Infinite Intelligence, perceived consciously or not. This is distinct from an individual's database of memory, or personal thought.

I will sometimes in the text refer to Mind as Source, to distinguish it from our human intellect. For example, "Mind" referred to in the three principles of "Mind, Consciousness, and Thought" refers to Source. Capitalizing "Center," as in "Center to circumference," also refers to Source, the realm of the Absolute, or the Tao, the Everything and No Thing out of which all things are formed.

These realms can be referred to but not actually explained, since our third-dimensional life experience is formed *from* them. We can point to these realms with words yet not really talk about them, as anything we could speak or write about them in words would be less than what they are.

The capitalization of these certain words through the printed text is my way of pointing to this never-changing, ever-flowing realm of Being.

CHAPTER 1

A Radical Idea

"You come to it through earnestness. Seek a clear mind and a clean heart. All you need is to keep quietly on it, inquiring into the real nature of yourself. You are what you are seeking."

—NISARGADATTA MAHARAJ

THE MESSAGE FOR THOSE OF YOU WHO ARE interested in integrating into your awareness *The Inward Outlook* paradigm is essentially that you can experience a happy life. This is not to imply that you will escape the inevitable challenges of day-to-day living. Rather it implies that while interfacing with these challenges in an inward outlook manner, you will be able to transcend life's vicissitudes by inwardly tapping into your own bottomless well of grace, ease, and hope.

The concept of achieving true happiness has seemed like a radical idea, elusive and mysterious to people for centuries. And the principles underlying an inward outlook approach are not new—they are to be found in some of the oldest spiritual disciplines available. However, *The Inward Outlook* paradigm translates age-old spiritual law into understandable language for the Western intellect. In this sense, East not only meets West but blends with West.

Principles are constant and reliable. Learning to integrate them into our own evolution of consciousness allows for developing deeper layers of understanding. At this juncture in our evolution, more and more people are actively seeking a deeper understanding of what lies behind the creation of our life experience. Many are thirsting for ballast, as the old ways of manipulating the third dimension fail to produce fulfillment.

The Inward Outlook paradigm reveals the thinking that leads to suffering and the thinking that leads to happiness. In this approach, there are two channels or types of thought: one is *analytical* thinking, which is memory, or data from the past, stored in the intellect, and the other is *free-flow* thinking, which is insight that emerges when being present in the moment with no attention paid to thinking from the past. Insights emerge from listening for what we *don't* know.

Neither modality is bad or good, although without understanding, getting caught in analytical thinking can lead to suffering, while the utilization of free-flow thinking can lead to happiness—the latter being referred to in this study as "the attitude of transformational humor."

The manifestation of an attitude of happiness is often expressed as a nice feeling, a feeling of lightheartedness. The higher the mood level, the more open and willing a person is to seeing the best in themselves and others. The principles underlying *The Inward Outlook* paradigm point the way toward identifying the factors that will lead to a life of happiness, compassion, and positive transformational change.

Organizations are particularly interesting to consider, as they are where most of us have spent a good part, or all, of our work life. Organizations are not just structures for accomplishing business results. Organizations are essentially people working with people to produce a particular result, and as such they are representative of many groups of people. Organizations are a microcosm or macrocosm of cultures, communities, and/or families.

When organizations successfully integrate *The Inward Outlook* paradigm into their structure, they evolve into healthier cultures. These organizational cultures are high-performing, person-centered learning environments, where personal core values align with the organizational vision and mission. Such organizations inevitably produce appreciative environments for their employees, quality products, high customer satisfaction, and creative problem-solving technologies.

It is inevitable that the cultural structure of such an organization becomes more hopeful, productive, and "light," with a noticeable lack of drama and conflict. And with such a reduction in conflict, a wellspring of effortless positive change emerges.

The path for teaching *The Inward Outlook* in business, as well as other environments, could be to simply add an emphasis on well-being, with the leaders of the business or community grounded in their own happiness and welfare. The impact of such an environment would be not only intellectually understood but also viscerally palpable.

Through their presence alone, these leaders would model health and compassionate humor in such a way that the participants would end up learning through nonverbal cues, as well as concrete examples. The result would be an energetic transference of empowering lightheartedness.

The implication for such organizations extends outward to the possibility of becoming model leadership communities. Such a leadership community demonstrates the potential for people working together harmoniously toward a self-actualized organization, in which every person assumes responsibility for the success of the organization and an integrated, harmonious culture.

Imagine an organizational culture—or family, or neighborhood—whose core values are compassion and synergy, mutual respect and brotherhood, service and happiness. How would the participants of such an environment operate? How would it impact these participants' lives outside the organizational or family culture? How then would these cutting-edge groups impact *other* cultures?

The Inward Outlook offers a path and a vehicle through which this kind of evolutionary transformation can take place in organizational structures of any kind. In some respects, this perception has been ahead of its time. In other respects, it is now perched on the threshold of current needs. People are hungry for a sense of meaning in work, and the old command-control management hierarchy does not serve the current, more conscious need for self-actualization and contribution.

What we need is a shift in perspective—a shift that will allow individuals to access those natural and effortless states of well-being and synergy generated by a compassionately humorous outlook.

As all types of organizations—*businesses, families, communities, school systems, etc.*—foster the kind of environment that we are describing, like-minded teams and leaders at all levels whose leadership is empowered from within (inward) and is expressed (outlook) for the good of all become the norm.

Such a shift in perspective will allow people to access those natural and effortless states of well-being generated by a compassionately humorous outlook.

The culture would transform because the transformed culture would exist within each individual. Each individual would bring the transformed culture with them, from the inside out, Center to circumference.

That's very powerful.

Notes

Notes

Notes

CHAPTER 2

A Principle-Based Paradigm

Stillness is your essential nature.
What is stillness? The inner space or awareness in
which the words on this page are being perceived and
become thought. Without that awareness, there would be
no perception, no thoughts, no world.
You are that awareness, disguised as a person.

—ECKHART TOLLE

IN THIS CHAPTER, WE WILL LAY DOWN the structure of how thought creates our reality. Once this is grasped, a fundamental shift in perception is available, allowing for choice to become more conscious. Human beings are thinking creatures, and we are consistently creating our experience of reality through choice, whether we realize it or not. All day long we choose which thoughts receive our attention. What we focus our attention upon is what we think about; what we think about is what we experience and, eventually, what manifests. We are all therefore masters of our experience of life.

The impact of understanding the role of thought is that we become masterful in *consciously choosing* what thoughts *get our attention*; thus we become more consciously masterful in creating the life experience we desire.

✳ The Law of Thought

Mind, Consciousness, and Thought, characterized by Sydney Banks, are the three principles that create our personal reality—referred to here as "principles" because they are the *constants* through which human beings form their individual and collective reality. *Principle* is defined by Webster as "a comprehensive and fundamental law; a primary source."

There is an operational relationship between the principles of Mind, Consciousness, and Thought, and it is important to understand how they work together to create each person's day-to-day reality. We could think of the interrelationship of these three principles as the structure through which the personality we know ourselves to be is not only created but expressed. There are other ways we could endeavor to talk about this interrelationship, though whatever words we choose are insufficient for truly expressing what we are attempting to capture.

In actuality, there is one Source, one Substance out of which all things are formed. We will distinguish the process of how thought manifests our experience in order to make clear our intellectual understanding. Again, these three principles are referred to as "principles" because they are the *constants* through which human beings form and experience individual and collective reality.

MIND, as we use it here, is the Power Source. It is the Source of Consciousness and Universal Thought, projected out together to ultimately form each person's perception and experience of reality through thought.

Mind is the One Substance out of which *all things* are formed. Words and personal thought are things. Since words and personal thought are things of form, they also emerge *from* Mind and therefore do not exist as form *in* Mind.

Form emerges from the Formless. Thought is the vehicle through which the Formless becomes form, according to the character of the thought.

Since words come from Mind, they are less than the totality of it. Therefore, words can refer to Mind but cannot directly capture its essence.

CONSCIOUSNESS is that which brings thought to life. It is the movement of Mind through us. In part, we experience Consciousness as our senses, although it is more than this.

Consciousness creates the sensory data in our day-to-day experience. It is the ingredient that gives thought the appearance of reality. Consciousness is the capacity to be aware of existence.

THOUGHT is the conduit for human evolution. It is the vehicle through which our experience is formed.

Universal Thought is the realm of Infinite Intelligence, which exists in the formless realm of Mind. "Infinite Intelligence" refers to the infinite knowledge available to all sentient beings, according to our level of understanding, and our developed ability to listen from being completely present in the moment, with no attention paid to thinking from the past.

The capacity to be completely present in the moment allows for what is often referred to as "flow," the free-flow conduit of thought. Flow thinking is the channel through which Infinite

Intelligence, or Universal Thought, is available to personal conscious awareness.

As we practice listening from this present moment thinking, we have more and more access to Universal Thought, which gives more profound levels of understanding life experience. We develop the capacity for more expanded perceptions of, and accessibility to, the ballast of compassion, forgiveness, common sense, and wisdom.

Personal thought is a person's current and accumulated cognitive perception of life, as well as their cultivated capacity to perceive the infinite levels of intelligence available from Source, or Mind. Personal thought does not exist as personal thought in the Formless Mind. Personal thought is form, emerging from the Formless as the characterized form of an individual's perceptions.

Personal thought determines our personal experience of our individual reality, based on the content of our thoughts and formed according to the character of our thoughts. Therefore, each individual's experience of reality is a direct result of the character of his or her thinking.

Genius is the result of a willingness to listen from Flow, to allow the undifferentiated consciousness of Infinite Intelligence to emerge as thought. Genius thinking brings into human awareness what occurs to us as "new thought" or "new creative expression" and thus often contributes to elevating the consciousness of humanity.

Mind, Consciousness, and Thought work together in concert, generating each person's day-to-day experienced reality, much the same as the basic elements found in chemistry interact to create compounds resulting in material form.

The word *element* is defined as "anything that is part of a compound or complex whole and connotes irreducible simplicity." There are a finite number of elements from which compounds are formed. All compounds can be reduced to the basic elements. All experience can be reduced to the three principles of Mind, Consciousness, and Thought, and these three principles, or elements, create the psychological compounds that we know as our personal reality. Said another way, everything we think about is a compound of these elements.

Mind, Consciousness, and Thought are constants, all working in sync within an indivisible relationship. Personal thought is the variable in the equation, because it is the character of the personal thought content that varies from person to person.

The varied content of an individual's thinking creates the distinctions in each person's psychological reality and gives the appearance of separateness. Separateness is actually illusion, as every person's psychological and physical reality is formed through the common thread of the interrelationship of these three principles.

Our unification—or Oneness—lies in the Formless being the Source of All.

∗ Levels of Understanding

"Levels of understanding" refers to the extent of our awareness of the fact of thought, which is that we are thinking creatures.

It also refers to the extent of our awareness of thought as a *function*, meaning thought is one of the variables in the three principles' interrelationship, or structure, that creates our experience of reality. The way in which we perceive the world and our quality of life improves as we understand the role of thought as a function.

In other words, "levels of understanding" refers to the depth at which we understand *that* we think, and that thought creates our experience of day-to-day life.

As this understanding deepens, we frequently find ourselves full of gratitude and compassionate humor, realizing that feelings are simply a physical experience of any state of mind out of which we operate.

"Levels of understanding" also refers to an ever-expanding awareness of consciousness, which recognizes that the perception of external reality is the result of personal thought. Therefore the truest interventions take place *inwardly*, in the realm of thought. We begin to understand that there is no true action in the outer material world. True action takes place in thought. Actions taken in the material world are all *reaction* to thought.

This perspective allows for a kind of freedom that comes from recognizing the illusion of the external world. Such lighthearted perspective enables you to walk into the midst of challenges and address serious issues and circumstances without the encumbrance of *feeling* serious. Instead you can operate with the empowering qualities of hopefulness, common sense, and compassion.

During the mid-1990s while I was teaching *The Inward Outlook* in my private practice as well as in my professional life as a public speaker and consultant, I was also interning as a psychology doctoral candidate. In the clinic where I worked, my colleagues and I partnered in pairs, co-leading fifteen schizophrenic patients five hours each day, typically three days a week.

The psychiatrist who was the medical director of our clinic, which treated the county's most persistently mentally ill patients, became quite frustrated with me for being so "idealistic" with my patients. He said I was not reality-based enough to be able to assist them. I replied as respectfully as I could that perhaps he was right, but my perspective was to look for the possible best in every patient in order to elicit the same from them, in spite of their presentation.

During this period, I had a patient in her late thirties whom I will call Elaine. Elaine was diagnosed with paranoid schizophrenia. Previously, Elaine had been in a board and care home for some time after her family determined they could no longer care for her.

Initially, her speech was very pressured—intense and staccato—and for the first several sessions, she repeated the same litany, staring at the floor. She talked about how people were following her, certain they would jump out of the bushes on her walk home and terrified that they would kill her. She had evidently told this fear to her previous therapists, including her psychiatrist, who all told her that this fear was an ungrounded fabrication and a delusion of her illness.

It struck me, after listening to her repetition of this fear for a couple of sessions, that no one who had treated her had actually ever validated her concerns or ever really listened to her.

Elaine aspired to finish high school, get her GED, and live independently. Her psychiatrist told her that this goal was not possible and that she would never get any better than her current state of mental health.

On my third session with Elaine, I decided to listen to her fears from the stance of possibility. Horrible things do happen to people; people are victims of crime and do get ambushed and harmed, sometimes for no reason. So I said to her, "Elaine, I believe you that this is possible." This stopped her in her tracks. She looked up at me for the first time in three sessions, mouth open in wonder. "I believe you," I repeated. "This type of situation *could* happen." I let that sink in.

For the first time, Elaine stopped telling her story and listened attentively. "But here's the problem," I said. "You are thinking about this happening so much that you never let yourself have a moment's peace. And the fact is, it hasn't happened to you at this point. So what if you were to stop paying so much attention to the *fear* of it happening and started paying attention to what you are *interested* in *having* happen?" I went on to say that if something frightening did happen, which could happen to any one of us, that she would have to deal with it at the time—but in the meantime, she could actually begin to enjoy her life and start to create the life experience she wanted.

Elaine never brought up that litany again. Over the next six months, we worked together an hour a week, and by the time our sessions together were complete, Elaine had moved out of the boarding home to live on her own. Once again she began seeing her father on a weekly basis, going out with him for hamburgers and milkshakes. When I followed up and asked about her, six months after our work together, I was told she had begun studying for her GED.

I never read the clinical reports on my patients until after I met with them, because I didn't want my initial assessment to be contaminated by the previous clinicians' diagnoses. As a result of allowing myself to "not know," I was able to perceive possibilities with these patients that very likely wouldn't have occurred to me had I beforehand assumed the reality of accepted clinical diagnoses and reports. Of course, I read the reports later, but I had by then been able to bring my own fresh perspective to whatever diagnosis was written, thereby achieving some very unusually positive results with patients previously diagnosed as people who would never improve.

Interestingly enough, my work with these patients was very effective. Their mental health, social skills, and community participation so improved that a year later the same medical director who had earlier been frustrated with my approach requested supervision from me with his patients. At that time he also requested further coaching on *The Inward Outlook* paradigm.

If the external world is indeed reality/illusion born of thought, many of our reactions to the external world are misguided. Again, true transformation lies within the realm of thinking, not in the apparent challenge or hopelessness of a given circumstance.

To reiterate, Mind is the Power Source. Consciousness neutrally does its job of breathing life into thought, according to the character of the thought. Essentially, Consciousness doesn't care what thought it brings to life; it has no value judgment. These three principles working together simply give the appearance of reality to whatever thought is presented.

Experience, then, is a reaction to thought. As stated above, the only true action takes place in thought. Hence, what we think is what we experience.

Forty years prior to the work of Mr. Banks, the great metaphysician Frederic Keeler identified these three principles as well, expressed through his own differing terminology. He referred to the cooperation of their interrelatedness as "The Law of Thought."

> *When the consciousness moves, we know this motion as thinking. To pre-determine the state of consciousness, the particular condition of thought in itself, is to pre-determine the concepts it shall receive and those it shall speak forth. This is a tremendous truth.*
>
> —FREDERIC KEELER

Conditioning the consciousness, through meditation practice or practicing the Presence of being in the moment with no attention to thinking from the past, predetermines the mindset or the kind of thinking the consciousness will receive. This then determines the way a person perceives and experiences their life and its circumstances.

The operational relationship between the three principles is thus, essentially, what Keeler calls "The Law of Thought." Because the three principles operate as a neutral law, the difference for humanity lies in our awareness and understanding of this law.

Understanding the operational relationship between the three principles allows for a life of well-being and happiness and a more refined and accessible sense of humor manifested as transformational humor.

As a result, one then gains freedom from the illusion that anything in the physical, emotional, or psychological realm can impact our common sense, serenity, or peace of mind.

Notes

Notes

CHAPTER 3

Thought:
Developing Conscious Choice

Listening to the Known or the Unknown

All is Chosen.
All choice is valid.
That choice will occur is a Universal Truth.
However, why a choice is made is a personal truth.
It is powerful to remember that our personal choices
determine the quality of our life experience.

—LAURA BASHA

As WE HAVE BEEN DISCUSSING, THE VARIABLE in the equation of
the three principles is personal thought, which varies according
to the character of an individual's thoughts. So for purposes of
clarifying its creative process of manifestation, we can describe

thought as being delineated into two distinctive qualities—one allowing access to personal thought alone, the other allowing access to Universal Thought, or Infinite Intelligence, which can also include personal thought. A brief discussion of these two distinctions in thought can awaken a fundamental shift toward consciously choosing where to focus your attention.

There are two modes of thought common to every human being: in-the-moment thinking, listening for and being available to insight, and analytical thinking, listening to memory and what is already known from the past. Some of the most helpful distinctions between these two modes of thought can be seen through defining them, as well as through understanding the particular attributes of each.

Understanding these two capacities of thinking available to people enables us to better sustain hopefulness and a sense of possibility in the face of personal, group, organizational, or global pressures and changes. People then continue to expand their creative thinking, improve productivity in all areas of endeavor, and tap into intrinsic motivation.

Sustaining hopefulness is achieved through the maintenance of a lighthearted attitude in spite of circumstances. This is an attitude that maintains possibility in the face of even dire circumstances, and it is the result of choosing to cultivate an alignment with Presence, or being present in the moment.

Such an optimistic outlook may leave us concerned that we are being unrealistic, in denial, or "Pollyannaish." However, it is in the balance of accessing analytical thinking while aligned with present moment thinking that gives human beings the ballast of wisdom coupled with a commonsense choice for action.

✳ Analytical Thought

Analytical thought describes a way of thinking that is limited, as it is based in the past. Analytical thinking is entirely made up of memory that is stored in the intellect as data. This is very much related to the way a computer stores data that has been entered.

The use of memory is essential, for without memory, most of our day-to-day tasks would have to be relearned each time there was a need for them. Imagine having to relearn how to use your phone every morning or relearn how to operate the car or balance the checkbook every time you used them. Clearly analytical thinking is a very useful and necessary tool, as memory is what allows us to navigate much of the logistical necessities of everyday living.

However, analytical thinking can become problematic when it is used exclusively, because it is entirely process-oriented. This use of thinking can contribute to continuous repetition of thoughts or ongoing reorganization of previously held ideas, when what is needed is insight or inspiration.

Since an individual's analytical thinking is relegated to memory only, and thus limited to what is stored, there can be a lack of freshness and insight. Exhaustion and depletion can result due to the arduous nature of having to remember and retrieve past information for any purpose, particularly when what is needed actually doesn't exist where we are looking!

You can experience a sense of boredom because when you are thinking solely from an analytical perspective, you are not in the present moment but rather distracted with thinking based in the past, although it probably doesn't occur that way. Consequently, your intellect is racing faster than your life, meaning it's not connected to what is actually happening in the moment, so there is no experience of appreciation, renewal, or creativity.

A heaviness, or lack of joy or presence, can occur when we focus only from an analytical mindset. As we review the past over and over, there is a tendency to worry. The thought of needing to figure things out or how to make things happen through accessing memory can create a feeling of hopelessness and burden.

Analytical thinking can be judgmental, since it compares and contrasts one memory to another; it can feel weighted with importance and significance, since *it has no recognition of itself as thought*. Because of this, everything can appear to have evaluative meaning and can be personalized since we are viewing life through a grid of past personal experience and personal memory.

Emotional reaction and reactively taking actions that in retrospect were not helpful can seem to make sense when focusing from the analytical mode of thought.

* Present Moment Thought

The free-flowing way of thinking is a natural state of consciousness inherent within each of us. It is the quality of thinking available to us when we are present in the Now. This thinking is the vantage point from which we have access to wisdom, creativity, genius, and an ever-present quiet mind.

Present moment thinking allows for more and more insight into the nature of the role of thought, ever deepening our level of understanding of how human beings function. It is natural, effortless, and exceedingly practical, as it also delivers commonsense input particular to any given situation at hand.

Listening to and from the best possible thinking we have access to at any given time connects us to the source of lightheartedness and compassion. We can deal pragmatically with serious situations without feeling serious. Due to the inherent wisdom and creativity of this quality of free-flow thinking, you feel able to trust your own ability to navigate any circumstance regardless of familiarity with the conditions.

The attributes of common sense, insight, and well-being arise because thinking from the present moment simply allows the appropriate thought and solution to occur. Consequently you don't wrestle or argue with your own reasoning processes.

Inspired thought subsequently occurs as an insight. The best way to advance is then unrestricted and coupled with a feeling of delight or compassionate humor experienced as gratitude. Learning to give up always trying to figure things out, you become comfortable with not knowing. You develop a capacity to listen for insight and for what you haven't previously been seeing.

Present moment thinking, or thinking that arises from Infinite Intelligence, is the most efficient thinking to utilize, as it takes the least emotional toll due to its stress-free nature. It is nonjudgmental and impersonal in that it assigns no motive and recognizes anything unlike itself as thought relegated to memory.

Memory, which is thinking from the past, actually doesn't exist until we give it our attention. It is our attention to thought that brings it to life.

Once a person recognizes that their thinking is from the past, they are actually in the present moment of Now, for it is only in the present moment that memory is recognized as past thinking. Memory, analytical thinking, has no recognition of itself as thought, since it is a closed data system perceiving itself to be a whole and complete reality.

As soon as we recognize we are caught up in memory, we are actually in that moment not paying attention to memory but rather paying attention to the insight of noticing memory. We can choose in that split second to continue paying attention to analytical thinking or shift our attention to what is happening in the present moment, removing all attention to the past.

This practice cultivates a pattern of how to choose consciously what you want to be experiencing, allowing you to express from authentic *being*. Such practice itself is simple, though there is the true work involved of *remembering*—remembering to notice when you are caught up in past reflection.

Present moment thinking allows for the use of analytical thinking in an appropriate way. It gives you the opportunity to make use of the things learned in the past through an in-the-moment approach of ease and effortlessness. Again, analytical thinking is necessary. Without it you would have to relearn very common everyday tasks. However, use of known data alone keeps you boxed in; the best you can do is travel in circles with only the illusion of change because, essentially, your experience of life becomes a continual review of the past.

The easy and diffuse way of present moment thinking is like a river that is always moving, always bringing fresh and refreshing ways in which to interact with your life experience. Because it does not infer motive, it does not personalize experience—which allows for compassion and understanding, even for those people and circumstances that appear harsh and demanding. To be grounded in a present-moment mindset brings with it peace of mind and wisdom, no matter the circumstance or condition.

Living from this effortless way of perceiving elicits resilience, good humor, and a tenderness toward yourself and others that doubles as a buffer to difficulties and misunderstandings. You maintain your equilibrium and make choices that are best for all concerned, staying open to an ever-continuing influx of fresh insights and feelings of well-being.

It becomes clear and obvious that the direction of health is toward the quiet stillness within the flow of the present moment. Within this quietness, this Silence, wisdom meets every need with order, harmony, and ease, and all needed adjustments take place.

Much like a tuning fork, the finer vibration of Infinite Intelligence transmutes any thought of denser vibration into its

Divine Correspondent: fear becomes Love, anxiety becomes Peace, judgment becomes Compassion. Practicing being completely present to what is happening in the Now, completely accepting the current circumstance or condition or problem, brings peace of mind.

With peace of mind comes a very high quality of thinking, which occurs as insight regarding the issue at hand. Drama in life diminishes, upset fades, solutions and the vitality needed to implement them become obvious and accessible.

Thinking from the present moment of Now gives direct access to the Formless: the reverberation of the One Substance. It is from our listening to the Silence that Infinite Intelligence is transmuted into our personal thoughts of wisdom, well-being, and joy.

❋ Feelings: The Indicator of Thought Quality

How does your experience express through you as feeling? If we consider analytical thinking, or memory, what does it feel like when you are thinking of the past, or when you rely on previous learning?

These feelings are often experienced as constraining in some form or other. They can be experienced as obviously constraining, like the frustration we feel while we impatiently sit in traffic, or while we search for missing car keys when we are already late for an appointment. Or the feelings can be more subtly constraining, like when we look for the missing five cents that would balance the checkbook, or when we reflect on finding the elusive perfect word to capture our thoughts.

Feelings are thoughts in motion; they are the way the body experiences thought. Sometimes we experience deep and powerful feelings that are overwhelming. If we allow ourselves to tolerate the feelings, they will eventually reveal themselves as cognition, as conscious thought, bringing relief and emerging as insight about deeper patterns or difficult circumstances.

The feelings could be those of love or joy or grief or anger or loneliness or frustration or contentment. By being willing to listen for the knowledge inherent within the feeling and developing a capacity to wait for the feeling to evolve into a conscious thought, we develop a powerful ability to awaken to our own innate authenticity, creativity, and genius.

Analytical thinking can also be experienced as very positive feelings, like when we are proud of our children performing in the school play. I remember one year when my seventh-grade daughter played Joan of Arc, and my third-grade son played Moses. This was the year when I was the mother of a saint and a patriarch! I was proud and delighted—great feelings, as I knew how much work had gone into the production, and my children were cool on that stage!

What's important to notice in the above example is that analytical mode feelings are always *contingent on something happening in the outer world*, in this case on my children's performance. It behooves us to learn how to recognize our own feelings that are characteristic of our analytical thinking, because, as stated previously, as soon as we recognize we are operating from memory, we are out of the analytical mode. We are instead in the present moment of free-flow thinking and pointed in the direction of possibility.

Analytical thinking cannot recognize itself. It has no outside vantage point from which to view itself. It is a closed data system of memory.

It is present moment thinking that recognizes our analytical thinking. The moment we recognize we are caught up in our thinking, we are actually free of the past, returned to the ease and wisdom of Now.

When my children's father died suddenly and too soon,

although the grief was profound, there were many moments in which the grief was experienced inside a greater feeling of love and gratitude for who he had been for all of us. The grief was contingent on the loss, while the love was noncontingent on the circumstance and was the ever-present realm inside of which our experience of loss was taking place. Being present to the love for him that was noncontingent on the circumstances allowed the grief to be tolerable.

Think of how you feel when you are truly relaxed and present, not paying much attention to your thoughts. Perhaps you are a musician completely caught up in the moment of fluidly playing a beautiful melodic piece, or you are simply listening to your favorite musical composition. Perhaps you are moved by the beauty of a sunset or by the tranquility of nature. Such feelings are expressions of the realm of the Now, and they are the result of being present to the truth of Being, which permeates nature and infuses beauty wherever you look.

Feelings experienced from the diffuse ease of the present moment can be referred to as "Divine Attributes of Source." By Divine Attributes, I mean what we might call higher-order feelings of Peace, Love, Harmony, Compassion, or Joy. Such higher-order feelings are not contingent on conditions or experiences happening in the outer world. They are the higher-order feelings intrinsic in the Eternal, the essence of who we really are.

Knowing that there are two modes of thought, two sources of thought to give our attention to and from which to choose to perceive life experience, brings freedom and power. Recognizing the difference between thinking from the past and thinking from the Now, the eternal source of Infinite Intelligence, is all that is required to return to the natural and effortless state of your own inner buoyancy.

The main work is *remembering* that there are two well-springs from which to think, the personal and the impersonal.

Practicing to consciously *choose* thinking from the impersonal is the *inward* avenue to the authentic *outlook* and positive essence expression that you are. Serene and powerful intrinsic leadership awakens you to your true purpose, inspiring you and your world, for the benefit of all concerned.

Notes

Notes

CHAPTER 4

Transformational Humor

Positive Transformational Change

*Flow with whatever may happen
and let your mind be free.
Stay centered by accepting
whatever you are doing.
This is the ultimate.*

—CHUANG TZU

SOMETIMES A SHIFT IN THOUGHT IS NOT perceived as thought but appears only as a shift in behavior. Through reflection on what we have been discussing, we can see that in spite of appearances, a shift in behavior is due to a shift in thinking.

As our understanding of this paradigm deepens, access to more refined and transformational levels of humor increases.

Increased understanding of thought as a function, as an operational relationship with Mind and Consciousness, increases the recognition of the illusory nature of life experience.

We are then empowered with an increased ability to experience a buffer from taking things personally, or taking things so seriously as to lose perspective or hope.

This does not mean to imply that serious issues don't arise in life or need to be addressed. Rather, it infers that as serious issues do arise and call for action, you can come from a state of mind that sees hopefulness, despite appearances to the contrary, and you can then address the serious circumstance from the clearest possible thinking.

We make our best choices from a clear, present moment state of mind, and this is coupled with a lighthearted or even inspirational feeling. Such feeling of hope comes from the sustained knowledge that a solution can be found. We can see through experience over time that hope is not contingent on the newfound solution but rather emerges from the inherent trust built through the consistent reliability of successful relevant solutions.

Transformational humor describes an aspect of humor elicited from what I will refer to as a "humor continuum." This humor continuum ranges from a baser, more cumbersome expression of humor that might be perceived as disrespectful, or an ironic sarcasm at another's expense; to jokes, fun, and comedy; to social and political humor; and to satire. The continuum then expands into transformational humor, moving from humorous expression into a compassionate perspective on life: a perspective of general optimism, possibility, and quiet contentedness. There emerges a childlike openness coupled with a wise and compassionate acceptance of the foibles of being a human on the physical plane. We begin to see what previously appeared as the only reality is actually the illusory quality of day-to-day life experience.

Over time, this perspective deepens into an unflappable sense of knowing that, in spite of all appearances and circumstances to the contrary, there is goodness and hope and an inherent order that moves toward positive change.

This above reference to the "humor continuum" refers directly to a person's continuum of understanding, or an individual's developed capacity to perceive how thought creates his or her experience of life.

Analytical thinking cannot recognize itself. It has no outside vantage point from which to view itself. It is a closed data system of memory.

It is the flow channel of thinking that recognizes analytical thinking. So as soon as we recognize we are caught up in our thinking, we are actually free of the past, returned to the ease and wisdom of Now.

It behooves us to update our definition of humor and increase our awareness and understanding of this paradigm that takes its cues from the inner Silence. What does the value of compassionate lightheartedness hold for all of us? In recognizing humor as a state of mind, this inquiry can demonstrate how such a mindset begins to create powerfully positive interactions and consequently a like-minded environment.

In any area of life experience, such an environment is fun, uplifting, and creative and is a compelling draw. An environment permeated with possibility and lightheartedness contributes to and actually creates positive transformational change.

Greeting life with inspired expectation and an understanding of the power inherent in being present in the moment augments the capacity for resilience and creates a less stressful experience of life. Such an attitude integrates your personal values with the choices you make. Anyone who values compassionate humor values health and well-being for self and others and realizes the connection between happiness and a fulfilled life experience.

A person's thoughts result in a person's attitude, which results in a person's choices, which result in a person's behavior. Integrating this logic into your own personal understanding lays a foundation within you for an increase in the experience of transformational humor and concurrent positive results.

The Inward Outlook is an inside-out approach to life. Implicit in its name is its impact. Simply through understanding the role of thought, and recognizing when you are paying attention to analytical thinking or memory, you can realize a healthy state of mind and experience the unfolding of authentic self-expression.

Positive transformational change describes movement that takes place in the direction of your purpose and vision for yourself based on core values personally meaningful to you. Goals would be met in healthy, lighthearted, and creative ways through actually living from the touchstone and ballast of authentic purpose. The actualization of these intentions in this way would constitute positive transformational change in any area of your interest.

It has been my experience from years of working with people from this inward outlook framework that people are able to access great reserves of resilience, common sense, and self-esteem when feeling hopeful. Once people begin to reclaim a sense of humor and hopefulness, creative thinking and pragmatic possibilities surface. This provides them with insight directly connected to the specific problem at hand, regardless of personality, condition, or circumstance.

It is compelling to distinguish how we can become more consciously aware of the source behind this transformational process. How do you become aware of the limitations that bind, and then become free of such limitations? And once aware, how do you address them in such a way as to be able to transmute them into strengths—use them as signposts that point you in the best direction to target the given problem? How do you use limitations to evolve into your inherently perfect self?

The longing is the promise of the fulfillment, for what else but longing for something would have you look? The problems are the precursors to the solutions. The questions are the precursors to the answers. It is the question that raises the possibility of hearing the answer. The question allows for the solution to be brought into conscious awareness.

How does humor play into this transformative process? You can notice that a lighthearted spirit contributes greatly to taking things less seriously, not avoiding serious issues but addressing them with a light tone. A consistent demeanor of happiness, shown in something as simple as an authentic smile, catches people's attention and curiosity. This consistency generates creativity and enthusiastic motivation toward a goal, no matter how challenging.

How can we maintain an attitude of happiness and well-being while walking into the fray day after day, and how can we not be contaminated by environmental issues?

The art of transformation lies in knowing that *the thought is the thing*. A transformational shift would be one in which a fundamental shift in perspective takes place. How can you take an inspirational and lighthearted insight and sustain it throughout a time-constrained and stressful day, and how do you then sustain it through the next day and the next so that it carries with it its own rejuvenation, building a new foundation upon which to greet not only your day but your world? And if you could develop this capacity, how impactful would it be, and in what way?

One common thread in having such a capacity does seem to be a deep sense of compassionate humor. Considering the possibility that there is a way to maintain clarity, lightheartedness, and peace of mind in the face of a seemingly or actually formidable life experience is a markedly different perspective from the habitual ways in which we have greeted it. Compassionate transformational humor intrinsic in this inward outlook paradigm unveils to us a supreme simplicity, previously masked by the intellect with an apparent mysterious complexity.

Transformational, compassionate humor dissolves struggle. It transmutes our thinking from attachment to the constraints of the personal into nonattachment, inviting the freedom and wisdom characteristic of the Impersonal.

Transformational humor is the capacity to be profoundly present while being joyfully childlike, infused with the wisdom of the elders.

Notes

Notes

CHAPTER 5

Purpose

A path is made by walking on it.

—CHUANG TZU

WHAT ARE YOU COMMITTED TO, AND WHAT lights you up? What is important to you, and what do you truly want? What would you like to generate for yourself and others? Finding the answers to these questions provides access to the touchstone of your authentically true self.

Before understanding the power of our thinking, we tend to see our circumstances as the externals that influence outcome. Consequently, our life may appear contingent upon externals: people and their opinions or the daily conditions of finances, health, relationships, or work issues. This thinking can extend further to include societal pressures, environmental issues, your status or educational background, and even the state of the stock market. We tend to take our cues about how we are doing and how things are going based on what's happening around us and outside of us.

As a result, we tend to personalize events, situations, and comments made by others, taking them with great seriousness. If our experience of life was, in fact, generated externally, it would make sense to analyze what is happening externally, to figure out how to deal with it. Of course, we can only do this from memory; we can only analyze using what we know from the subjective past, and this frame of reference tends to create feelings of seriousness, heaviness, and worry.

Even though we now recognize the deeply creative and powerfully affirmative state of mind that arises from being present in the moment, and how tapping into it results in feelings of well-being, timelessness, and ease, through education and enculturation we learn to turn away from our natural ability to embrace joy and fulfillment. The educational and societal learning process focuses more on memory than staying in the present moment of creative flow thinking.

The value of *The Inward Outlook* paradigm is that it illumines the interplay of the underlying principles of the role of thought so that we can understand how to rekindle the excitement and enjoyment of life that is naturally available to us.

As we have seen, a "light" perspective contributes to positive transformational change. This optimistic outlook sets the stage for having a gentle approach to challenging issues, allowing for new possibilities and ways of perceiving to unfold. Coming from a place of resilience and openness to change creates a state of mind that is free from concern or discomfort.

Without this inward outlook, we tend to get caught in the illusion that external experience is happening *to* us, rather than realizing that our external experience is reflective of our own internal and individual perspective.

When our thinking relies on memory alone, it gets off track about the outer circumstances. We then make insecure choices based on erroneous assumptions that appear logical and justified. We tend to become victims of our own misguided thoughts. We make up stories about what past experiences meant, and we live from those interpretations, as if they were the truth. Without understanding how thought creates our experience of life, without seeing the availability of inspired thinking inherent in the eternal present moment, each of us is at the mercy of our conditioned thinking and personalized memory.

"Understanding" is not simply the intellectual grasping of the logic of *The Inward Outlook*. The paradigm is not simply a formula of Mind + Consciousness + Thought = Reality. What is meant here by "understanding" is the insight that comes from recognizing *how* your personal thought creates your personal experience, as well as *how* impersonal Thought operates as a *function*. Impersonal Thought operates as a *function*, as a universal law, in operational relationship with Mind and Consciousness.

This kind of understanding results in a shift in our perspective toward experience, recognizing the illusory nature of form. When we understand that form manifests as a result of the Universal Law of Thought, according to the character of the thought, we experience life less personally, less reactively.

We see clearly not only *that* experience is perception but also *how* experience is perception. We participate in life experience yet with the buffer and wisdom of being a compassionate observer.

How do we stay connected to this compassionate lightheartedness? How do we remember that our experience of life is essentially all made up, that it's all arbitrary?

One powerful method of accessing this positive and effective frame of mind is through understanding personal purpose.

Purpose captures the heart and core of your essence and is the highest expression of yourself. What is the vision you have for expressing your most authentic self? This is the true self that you dream you could be but are afraid you cannot.

Practicing being present, in the moment, with no attention to thinking from the past, provides you with access to the ballast of your personal purpose. Such practice awakens you, through the experience of your own essence and your authentic and self-actualized way of being in the world. This way of being in the world is you living your purpose, in any moment and circumstance of your life.

Recognizing the general inauthentic perspectives we can innocently have of ourselves before we begin to reflect on the essence of who we truly see ourselves to be is a first practical step in perceiving authentic purpose. It's important to acknowledge that the invalidating internal conversations we all experience are part and parcel of being human. Examples of such negative internal dialogue are "I'm not good enough" or "I don't deserve to have that" or "I can never get that right," etc., etc., etc.. These invalidating statements occur within every one of us.

Such thoughts become particularly audible when you are in the conscious process of practicing to recall and return to your true self. When you hear these internal falsehoods, practice acknowledging to yourself that they are the seductive attempts of your protective false personality, whose reason for existing stems from the belief in survival.

The egoic self, or false personality, wants to convince you that you need to be kept "safe" from feelings of fear and perceived vulnerability. In actuality, these are internal phrases integrated into your psyche by your own interpretation and acceptance of past events. Focus on this background commentary keeps you—consciously or unconsciously—from evolving into the freedom of true self-expression, expressing your true personality. Listening to these invalidating conversations keeps you from realizing yourself as your purpose.

Any inspired thought that prompts you to commit to something bigger than yourself allows you to be your true purpose. Such a thought captures the essence of not only what you want for your own life but also what you want available to all of humanity.

How do we give birth to that authentic self-expression which also has the power to catalyze such possibility in others?

Within the journey of becoming our optimal selves, we must be willing to deal with those above-mentioned invalidating conversations, because they are sure to become very loud as we move ourselves toward being positive contributions. ·

This is the true work—walking through the fires of the internal crucible that ultimately provides for our long-desired transformation. During this process, it is often helpful, although not essential, to have a guide who has dealt with these issues personally, empowering them to assist you as a coach. The key is to *identify* and *express* your true self, which is you as your purpose. Listen from that inner prompting of your wisdom, and allow for the truth inherent in its authenticity to inform you of your choices.

As we keep listening and keep checking in to see if the inner perceptions are aligned with who we aspire to be, we watch our thinking morph and refine. Being present to the inner invalidating monologue, and turning our attention away from it, allows us to hear the essence expression of our own ever-evolving authenticity.

The outcome of this work results in an awakened awareness of what you might call your "true north," that resonating inner sense of authenticity and vitality. That inner compass serves to keep you on track in times of doubt, stress, and confusion.

Who you aspire to be that moves you is who you truly are. In the process of awakening to this insight, anything less than the representation of who you truly are begins to become apparent. Instead of automatic choices, you have an opportunity to make conscious choices.

When challenged by life, you can find your way back to authenticity through an internally focused question: *What would I, living from purpose, acting from the perspective of this authentically expressed woman/man that I am, think or do in this situation, in this condition, or in this relationship?*

Personal purpose emerges from a deep listening for what you are truly aligned with, committed to, and passionate about. It is an expression of the inherent integrity of your life—your raison d'être. Distinguishing and expressing yourself as purpose results from alignment with Center—the stillness of the present moment—to the circumference of your world.

You can, and many people do, write a statement that is your personal purpose. However, who you are as purpose is bigger than any words can communicate. Who you are as purpose is also bigger than any one action you can take or be committed to. Such words and actions can certainly be authentic expressions of your purpose, yet they alone cannot capture the entire realm of who you are as purpose.

✳ *Personal purpose is Essence expressed.*

From authentic purpose, the capacity to harness intention and power is exponentially increased. The result is an inherently synchronized person who is inspired to grow and who is infused with the vitality of awakening. Such self-perception cannot be overestimated in terms of its capacity to produce extraordinary results.

There is an underlying profound simplicity that emerges through alignment with your eternal essence. In the present moment, there is only the presence of being. From being, all needed intelligence emerges for any particulars in any given moment.

* Practice being the Presence instead of the person.

In the present moment, compassion for humanity is coupled with the oftentimes absurdity of life. We retain our lighthearted state of mind regarding circumstance while keeping our hearts open to the joys and travails of the physical plane.

The basic pivotal insight about an inward outlook is realizing the nature of thought. Once you awaken to how thought functions and evolves, the main work is remembering this. It is simple but not always easy, and it takes practice.

The goal is remembering that *the thought is the thing.*

Remember to essentially *stop thinking*, or stop *paying attention* to thinking from the past. This is actually practicing the ease and peace of mind of being present in the moment of now.

The realization of who you are at core—who you want to be as a presence in your world and what you want to bring to your life experience and to the experience of others—is you as your purpose. This statement could operate as a touchstone for remembering: *I am a creative spark of Source.*

Through claiming expression of yourself as purpose, you can distinguish the inauthenticities that you have made up for survival. By shining the light on these inauthenticities, you come to understand that, because of how you have been seeing life experience, you have been making certain choices that produce certain results that you do not want. This insight reveals that all it takes to facilitate change, to express authentically, is to get clear about what you want—who and how you want to be in the world—and consciously, through distinguishing what thoughts you are paying attention to, make choices consistent with producing those results.

All experience is the result of choice; everything is choice. Even if you don't agree with that statement, that is a choice. All is chosen.

To what thoughts are we choosing to pay attention? Are we cultivating a consciousness in alignment with who we are—present in the moment as our purpose?

Are we seeing the psychological innocence in others and realizing that everyone is doing the best they can, given the way they see life? Or are we defending our own perceptions, taking things personally, and thus feeling justified in reacting? If I am committed to actualizing world peace, how well am I keeping peace in my own family, my own relationships, my own internal emotional state?

Answering these questions takes something. Paradoxically it takes nothing, and yet it takes everything. The work is simple but not easy, for the patterning of our thinking has taken years, decades, perhaps lifetimes to set in place. We are born into cultural mindsets that we are not even aware of as thought. We are born into ways of looking at the world, differing global mindsets that are what we refer to as "differing cultures."

There are many beautifully different points of view and different aesthetics and different spiritual philosophies worth respecting and sharing and valuing in each other and in each culture. We can choose to see the beauty in these differences, appreciating the abundance of variable perceptions, or we can choose to feel threatened by differences, thinking they somehow challenge or invalidate our own points of view. One choice adds to peace and relatedness; one choice adds to discord, insecurity, and separateness.

Particularly as our world gets "smaller" with technology uniting us in ways that were inconceivable just a couple of decades ago, we want to become aware of the habitual limiting thinking that keeps us separate so that we can awaken to the commonality of humanity.

Living your purpose is simply being present in the moment with no attention to thinking from the past. You as your purpose will occur in whatever guise is needed at the moment. You don't have to mentally prepare for it. Being present allows for it to emerge. This inward outlook results in emanating who you are as an authentically expressed individual. It radiates purpose from you and infuses your world with all possibility.

Notes

Notes

Notes

CHAPTER 6

The Silence

There are no others.

—RAMANA MAHARSHI

ALL HEALING TRANSMUTATION TAKES PLACE in the Silence. Through the practice of quieting the thinking process, either through meditation or consciously stopping thinking, we can turn our attention away from the cacophony of incessant automatic thinking that passes through and practice listening to the quietness. Listen to and for the Silence; there is a resonance to It.

Listen for the profundity of the Silence. It has the resonance of vastness. Listen until you hear it; it is equally everywhere present and always available. We look at each other through it. Cultivate an affinity with the Silence of Source. It is the only ballast that we can depend on, and it requires no guru outside of yourself.

The Silence is the Guru, and it lives eternally through each of us, waiting to receive our attention so that it can find expression uniquely *as* us, every individual. All hopes are possible manifestations through cultivating this affinity with the Silence.

> *Never tell anyone they can't do something, for God may have been waiting centuries for someone who didn't know that.*
>
> —THE REVEREND KATHRYN JARVIS

There is an evolutionary benefit to cultivating a state of mind that is permeated with a deep and unflappable sense of knowing that, in spite of all appearances to the contrary, there is hopefulness and an inherent order which moves toward positive change.

Such knowing augments a life, no matter what the conditions. As you cultivate this intimacy with the Silence, there is a vibrancy of hopeful certainty that permeates your presence and is felt by others, elevating the mood however subtly. Elevation of mood is a direct indicator of elevation of the quality of thought.

Quality of thought is very important when considering the basic tenet of this paradigm, that thought creates your experience of life, what appears as reality. A healthy approach is a skeptical one that respectfully questions all possibilities to the contrary—that is, is there a place, an incident, or a condition where I cannot trace it back to thought? In my experience so far over these past decades, the answer continues to be no.

But don't believe me. Belief assumes veracity. You want to know. It is in the laboratory of your own life experience that you can test assumptions such as those posed here. It is only through the tempering and refining of yourself and living a life informed by listening to the Silence and its realm of Infinite Intelligence—testing the validity of the operational relationship of Mind, Consciousness, and Thought—that you can trust and know any certainty of its truth.

Inner questioning from sincere desire to understand is one way to develop. The questions themselves are the precursors to the answers. It is the answer, the realization or insight that desires to be revealed to conscious cognitive awareness, that is the catalyst for the question and so subsequently takes the form of the question. As this occurs, answers are unveiled, and understanding deepens.

This deeper understanding reveals how to keep your bearings and results in a serene demeanor and attitude, which affects the environment through which you walk. Just as the vibrational rate of a tuning fork initiates the same vibrational rate of sound in another tuning fork, alignment with the wisdom of the Silence allows us to flow within its lighthearted yet deep sonorousness. This catalyzes the same depth and lighthearted feeling in another, through the subtlety of ease. When something desirable comes through ease, there isn't much to resist—in fact, it's quite the opposite.

What gets catalyzed in another by a person who is aligned with the Silence is vibrant vibrational resonance. The thinking that is then awakened in that other person is insight that the other person is seeking. This is not a personal manipulation of any sort. Remember that the Silence is the realm of *Infinite Intelligence*. The resonance of the Silence, through someone aligned with the Silence, catalyzes the Silence in another, revealing the answers to the questions the other person is asking, even if those questions are not conscious.

They may think it's you that has awakened them. You want to know that it isn't you; it isn't that personal. In fact, the more we practice aligning with the Silence, the more authentic we become. We awaken to the peaceful simplicity and freedom of the ordinary. The resonance of alignment with the Silence is what catalyzes awakening in another.

There is a physics to it, a vibrational awakening that is gentle. It is irresistible in that it doesn't engage the personal thought process, but rather it awakens within a person the Impersonal Thought of Infinite Intelligence available to all human beings.

This Infinite Intelligence takes the form of whatever thought is needed to reveal the relevant solution, the answer to the query in which you or another is engaged. Nothing need be analyzed within yourself for such a solution. And for a person in the presence of someone aligned with the Silence, no words need be exchanged between the two for the other person to see a relevant solution to their own issue.

Alignment with the Silence may occur to you at first as a feeling of quiet contentment, or a feeling of being moved, or a feeling of joy, or even a feeling of deep longing. But this feeling is the awakening, which will—if not denied by you—eventually unfold as cognitive insight. Such is the power of cultivating an alignment with the Silence. It does the work through us— effortlessly, gently, always perfectly fulfilling whatever the need. Through gentleness you will develop trust in Infinite Intelligence to do its work, knowing that it will occur to the seeker as a relevant personal cognition. True power is the gentle expression of such a transference. Gentleness generates no resistance—it is irresistible, and therein lies its power.

This is why when you wonder what your purpose in life is, you can trust that you are living it when you are being present in the moment, awake within the Silence. You will be relying on the creative genius available to every human being, for you will know that allowing yourself to relax into a mental state of listening for "not knowing" allows for authentic expression of new insight to be heard.

A calmness will permeate your presence, because you will not be taking cues from the external circumstances but rather from an inward outlook that listens from the internal quietness of Mind. If Mind is All, then it is every thing and no thing and can take whatever form is needed to solve any problem.

We often say we want to "make a difference." Making a difference is at the heart of being a change agent, and true change agents take their cues from the Silence within. Change agents are not just relegated to the business world. Change agents are needed in every walk of life and at any age. They are habitually listening to what they don't know, because insight is the intervention needed in any system that says it wants to change.

A change agent is a person who has cultivated the capacity to deal with their own inner turmoil, frustrations, and inauthentic expressions of self and turned to the Silence for intuitive guidance. Such a person ongoingly does the true inner work needed to generate themselves as their purpose, their own authentic self-expression.

To have done this inner work is to have developed the capacity to act from being willing to be responsible for creating your experience of life. This is a powerful freedom and a gift to give yourself. A grace permeates someone who understands the innate freedom available through the willingness to be responsible for creating their own life experience.

This perceptual stance allows you to know that when walking into an environment that requires positive transformation, anything encountered that is less than harmonious or healthy is the manifestation of thought—nothing more. It is as real as any other thought or mindset, meaning that it is as illusory as any other thought or mindset. So you are, as the change agent, buffered from much of the impact of a negative or hostile environment because you are taking your cues from your internal well of wisdom, not from the situation at hand.

In effect, you then see the matrix behind life, and the psychological undercurrents of a situation. Without the understanding of the role that thought plays, the matrix can appear real. It is the knowing that life experience is a creation born of thought and is therefore illusory, though it *appears* real, which truly frees you to walk into any circumstance or condition and emerge perhaps not untouched, but unscathed.

With that freedom, you become influential in your environment due to the silent and irresistible catalyst quality born of a serene state of mind. We ought not to underestimate the true power of the gentleness intrinsic to the Silence.

The attitude expressed from the Silence is quietly contented and hopeful and delightfully anticipates the unexpected, allowing for people's mistakes without judgment. Operating from this gentle stance, you cast your own light, resulting in that light permeating the environment within which you walk. Your presence raises the feeling of the environment to one of hopefulness and calm. Your light—at home, at school, or in the office—is simply the luminosity of the quality of your thinking. It is all thought.

Since the physics of a higher vibrational rate catalyzes the lower vibrational rate of the instruments around it, the resonance of your state of mind when aligned with the resonance of the Silence catalyzes the health in yourself, in another person, as well as in an entire system. The unhealthy system cannot stay the same if a consciousness of health and compassion remain within it. This is true leadership.

Most of us are looking for such a way to walk through life. If you know that what you are seeing is simply one point of view, as valid as any other, and you are aware that there is a larger context within which everything fits, it is easier not to take to heart any perceived injustice over a circumstance or condition.

The Silence reverberates with the compassion of transformational humor. Bringing such compassionate lightheartedness to a situation—which we might also characterize as kindness—becomes more and more frequent, until an attitude of tenderness tends to be the habit.

Reaction, or taking experiences or others personally, greatly diminishes. Understanding how not to take anything personally is freedom. To not personalize experience while maintaining an attitude of compassion is to recognize that anything other than well-being and hopefulness is illusion. This is not to imply that life experience isn't difficult, tragic, or even unconscionably traumatizing at times, but such occurrences can now be held within the context of understanding that your responses to such experiences originate in thought. Experiencing gratitude in the midst of grief becomes possible; experiencing hope in the midst of fear becomes possible. This way of greeting life experience is transformational.

We want access to our own health, both psychological and physical. We are reluctant to embrace the idea of innate health and all its inherent possibilities because of the fear that what we so ardently desire in terms of authentic self-expression and happiness may actually be elusive and not come to pass. The potential for being disappointed—that perhaps we are not what we hope we could be—feels unbearable. So we fight to maintain the status quo of our familiar individual and separate realities, even if they compromise our peace of mind.

The self-actualized person is living from purpose, consistently listening from the Now, the internal wisdom of the Silence. The willingness to engage with the inner transmutation process, the willingness to address your own inauthenticities and your own inner egoic status quo, is a demonstration of your intention for generating your own power, leadership, and freedom.

This is the true work, and once undertaken, the Infinite Intelligence inherent in us as our authentic purpose *unfolds us*. Once you are aligned with this inner purpose, inspiring others occurs naturally. When you are present in the moment of now, you will naturally reverberate the qualities of the Silence.

One may seek out a coach to facilitate this process, though such a process could be facilitated only by someone who has walked through their own fires, as all such evolution takes place from Center to circumference.

When we come from this knowing of who we are as true self, we can be bold. The boldness comes not from fear or arrogance but from the confidence and clarity of listening with humility to inner wisdom.

Listening from inner wisdom catalyzes compassionate understanding. This protects the self-realized person, buffering them from the onslaught of past patterning of any invalidating mindset while bringing the possibility of transformation to that same mindset.

The intelligence which unfolds from affiliating with this lighthearted state of mind will inform you as to next steps and strategies, and those around you will naturally gravitate to their own health, accessing better solutions and ideas. The possibility is for a whole system to shift toward its purpose. Such a shift change will not be seen as difficult, threatening, or frightening but rather as taking the next logical steps needed to achieve whatever purpose has been intended or even articulated.

A self-realized person is a natural change agent. "Change agent" is one modern term for the true mystic. The true mystic wears no armband advertising such. And the true mystic, as a change agent, walks through all arenas of life: as homemaker, line worker, CEO, executive, poet, teacher, student, elder, child.

At any age, any gender, any role in life experience, any cultural or educational background, the true mystic emanates a serene countenance, listening from the cues of Infinite Intelligence, Omniscient Wisdom, and Omnipotent Love.

One with Silence is the majority.

Notes

Notes

CHAPTER 7

Being

There is no way home.
Home is the Way.
—THICH NHAT HANH

THE INWARD OUTLOOK IS A STATE OF MIND that is a conduit for positive, effortless change. The awareness of compassionate humor as transformational, which is a natural expression of this paradigm, brings a subtle but important shift of focus. Much like Wisdom, Compassion, and Humility are recognized as having within them all the necessary attributes for positive evolutionary advancement, Transformational Humor can be elevated to that same position of influence.

Identifying compassionate humor as its own state, we have access to it as a vehicle for understanding kindness and Joy.

Humor with compassion distinguishes its transformational influence and sets it apart in meaning from the other varied definitions of humor. We can then speak about it and have it influence the process of transformation in a more direct way.

What arises from this heightened awareness is the opportunity to focus on transformational humor in its own right, an attribute worthy of reflection due to its connection to well-being. Each is replete with ease and so offers an open path of least resistance.

The resonance of transformational humor's inherent peacefulness and healing integrates into the system of the physical body and into the psyche. As you consciously cultivate this alignment, the resonance of the integration emanates as a way of being in your world, in the world.

* *Being catalyzes Being.*

The hope here is that those of you who are interested in inculcating *The Inward Outlook* as a principle-based approach could practice it and test it out. From such personal research done within the laboratory of your own life experience, you could consequently validate and rely on the concepts presented here. You could then see new ways to bring to light for others the positive impact of understanding this way of being. The thought is the thing.

Through practicing this outlook, over time life experience becomes easier—not the circumstances so much but rather the capacity to address circumstances with less and less concern or struggle. There is more impact with less effort. Whether in navigating day-to-day living or through teaching or leading others, you will find the people in your life are relaxing around you.

More reflective conversations will come forth as people ask about your perspective or simply want to be around you. The ease generated by cultivating an inward outlook is contagious and compelling.

Much of this response has to do with your lack of judgment and an increased acceptance of others and their differing points of view, available simply from being present with them. More depth emerges in relationship, and fewer objections arise from the intellect. This is not to imply that people stop questioning, for questioning is essential to growth. However, people become more inquisitive in a respectful way, questioning expands into inquiry, which creates a fertile condition for the emergence of insight.

In this way we greet life experience listening for innate well-being from others, and through such listening, we elicit the same. We bring what we are looking for. This is being in the world, not of it, from which emerges clarity, confidence, and joy in self and others.

The results generated from a hopeful, positive feeling are infused with possibility. Using the concept of humor as a results-based approach from this inward outlook, you can more tangibly see the connection of this attitude affecting positive change in your own experience. You can see how hopeful perceptions of possibility affect choice, and consequently how your choices either accomplish or block your desired results.

The hopeful purpose of this book is to facilitate a shift in the thinking you have about the accessibility of lightness of spirit. Generally we have not perceived lightheartedness as easily available to ourselves or to our varied communities. Such possibility of positive change, of not only *making* a *difference* but being the difference we wish to see in our world, begins within our own thinking, Center to circumference.

You can awaken to your innate capacity for creating a fulfilling and joyful life experience. Deepening your understanding of the role of thought allows for ease in access to an attitude of compassionate and transformational lightheartedness. Realizing the power that you have intrinsically available to you through understanding the role thought plays in creating your experience is a life-changing intervention. You realize you have the capacity to lay a strong foundation for a contentedly serene life experience.

Alignment with the present moment of now leaves you with less to react to, less to resist, fewer feelings of defensiveness, and more openness to simply being profoundly present. This resonance takes the form of whatever is needed and generates within you a way of being in the world. You awaken to the truth that at the core of life, all is well.

> *All that we are is the result of what we have thought. . . .*
> *If a man speaks or acts with a pure thought, happiness*
> *follows him, like a shadow that never leaves him.*
> —GAUTAMA BUDDHA

Practicing *The Inward Outlook* paradigm results in a growth and developmental process which ongoingly unfolds us. Compassionate, transformational humor is a sense that we have as a gift, much like sight or hearing, though it is not a physical sense. It is not contingent on the world of form to have its impact. Its conception is in the realm of the Formless, so its transformational capacity lies in its ability to return us to Source.

An inward outlook informs a way of being in the world and reveals a doorway to peace, health, and happiness. It is ever available to you, and though it can be ignored, it cannot be extinguished. From cultivating alignment with its consistently reliable principles, you can remember what is real and true. Look at your world and others from the view of being Source. This is *The Inward Outlook*: possibility, fulfillment, peace, and joy.

The Practices Book for
The Inward Outlook:
Deepening Your Capacity
to Be Present

A PARADIGM FOR AWAKENING

A PRACTICES STUDY GUIDE IS INCLUDED IN this revised version of *The Inward Outlook*, to assist in deepening the understanding of the paradigm and thereby bring *The Inward Outlook* perspective to life in your everyday experience. It is a useful guide for individuals as well as for study groups, to facilitate exploring the implications of the teaching. We realize the true impact of these principles only when they become integral enough to be remembered during the routine ups and downs of life.

You will find that through the practice of these principles, an expanded creative freedom of expression emerges. You will feel grounded and confident in the newfound trust you have in your own innate wisdom and common sense. You will make choices that are more conscious and more in alignment with your core values.

The inquiry approach with chapter references can reveal areas in which you have gained understanding, as well as point out concepts that may require you to rethink a response or consider a new possibility. As you will see, many of the questions ask you to identify areas in your life to which you could bring practical application of the principles.

The inquiries will challenge you to step into your leadership capabilities and live into your true self-expression. This is a journey of growth that has no ending, and it can be expansively inspirational as you perceive pragmatic new ways of being in relationship with yourself, with others, and with your world.

The practices workbook is designed to be used as a reference guide, since it provides the chapter locations for the responses. How can you expand your own responses from the statements in the book text, in ways that make them more relevant to you?

Enjoy the process—have fun with it! There are no wrong responses! This practices book of inquiries is intended as an interactive way to open the door to expanded perception and greater fulfillment in life. Celebrate each moment as increasing clarity allows for your true genius, authenticity, and profound essence to emerge.

—Laura Basha, PhD, August 2022

THE PRACTICES

What is your understanding of a "paradigm"?

_____

_____

_____

_____

_____

_____

_____

_____

_____

What does "awakening" mean to you?

_____

_____

_____

_____

_____

_____

_____

_____

INTRODUCTION TO
THE PRACTICES

---

*The man with insight enough to admit his limitations
comes nearest to perfection.*
—JOHANN WOLFGANG VON GOETHE

THESE NEXT TWO QUESTIONS WILL HELP YOU to focus on areas in your life that you may want to transform. Keeping these in mind as you complete the rest of the workbook will help bring personal meaning and application to you.

Is there any area (or areas) of your life in which you would like to gain some insight?

_____

_____

_____

_____

_____

_____

_____

_____

Are there any areas of your life where you feel entangled or stuck and would like more freedom?

_____

_____

_____

_____

_____

_____

_____

_____

Now, bring your responses from above to the concepts identified in *The Inward Outlook*:

_____

_____

_____

_____

_____

_____

_____

One outcome of practicing an inward outlook is a shift in

_____ .

What would such a shift mean for you?

_____

_____

_____

_____

_____

_____

_____

How does transformational humor allow us to view life from a neutral stance? Please explain.

_____

_____

_____

_____

_____

_____

_____

_____

CHAPTER 1

A Radical Idea

"You come to it through earnestness. Seek a clear mind and a clean heart. All you need is to keep quietly on it, inquiring into the real nature of yourself. You are what you are seeking."

—NISARGADATTA MAHARAJ

What opens up for you in the statement: "By integrating your awareness of *The Inward Outlook* paradigm, you may escape the impact of the inevitable challenges of day-to-day living"? Please elaborate.

_____

_____

_____

_____

_____

_____

_____

_____

_____

_____

_____

Nisargadatta Maharaj is quoted as saying: "You are what you are seeking." How does this make sense to you?

_____

_____

_____

_____

_____

_____

_____

_____

_____

The principles underlying an inward outlook approach are found in the oldest spiritual disciplines. What does this mean for you in terms of application?

_____

_____

_____

_____

_____

_____

_____

_____

Is Truth a constant or does it change and alter? What is the impact of your answer in terms of how you live your life?

_____

_____

_____

_____

_____

_____

_____

_____

_____

_____

_____

_____

Organizations and corporations are not just businesses; they are made up of individual people representing many cultures, communities, and families. What does this mean to you in terms of your experience of organizations and how you interact with them?

_____

_____

_____

_____

_____

_____

_____

_____

_____

_____

_____

_____

Identify a few benefits that emerge when an organization integrates the principles of *The Inward Outlook*.

_____

_____

_____

_____

_____

_____

_____

_____

_____

_____

As you deepen your understanding of these principles, what are the ways in which you could positively influence your organization, your community, or your family?

_____

_____

_____

_____

_____

_____

_____

_____

_____

_____

CHAPTER 2

A Principle-Based Paradigm

Stillness is your essential nature.
What is stillness? The inner space or awareness in
which the words on this page are being perceived and
become thought. Without that awareness, there would be
no perception, no thoughts, no world.
You are that awareness, disguised as a person.

—ECKHART TOLLE

Human beings are thinking creatures. The average person thinks fifty thousand to seventy thousand thoughts per day, although most of them are not conscious. From an inward outlook perspective, what do you see when considering this fact?

_____

_____

_____

_____

_____

_____

_____

_____

_____

_____

MIND, CONSCIOUSNESS, and **THOUGHT** are the three principles that create our experience of reality. Please share in your own words your understanding so far of the principles.

_____

_____

_____

_____

_____

_____

_____

_____

_____

1: MIND

_____

_____

_____

_____

_____

_____

2: CONSCIOUSNESS

_____

_____

_____

_____

_____

3: THOUGHT

_____

_____

_____

_____

_____

_____

If the principles of Mind, Consciousness, and Thought are constants, what does this mean for your life experience?

_____

_____

_____

_____

_____

_____

_____

_____

_____

Mind, Consciousness, and Thought work together in concert. Please explain.

_____

_____

_____

_____

_____

_____

_____

_____

_____

_____

How would you describe Universal Thought?

_____

_____

_____

_____

_____

_____

_____

_____

_____

The capacity to be completely present in the moment is often referred to as "flow" thinking. What are some of the characteristics of this type of thought?

_____

_____

_____

_____

_____

_____

_____

_____

_____

How would you describe personal thought?

_____
_____
_____
_____
_____
_____
_____
_____
_____
_____

Understanding the operational relationship between the three principles allows for a life of well-being and peace of mind. In what ways would this impact your experience of yourself and your life?

_____
_____
_____
_____
_____
_____
_____
_____
_____
_____

Which is the "Power Source": Mind, Consciousness, or Thought? Please explain.

_____
_____
_____
_____

_____

_____

_____

_____

_____

_____

_____

_____

How does a deeper understanding of Mind, Consciousness, and Thought empower you in your life?

_____

_____

_____

_____

_____

_____

_____

_____

_____

_____

_____

CHAPTER 3

Thought:
Developing Conscious Choice

Listening to the Known or the Unknown

All is Chosen.
All choice is valid.
That choice will occur is a Universal Truth.
However, why a choice is made is a personal truth.
It is powerful to remember that our personal choices
determine the quality of our life experience.

—LAURA BASHA

What are the two distinct channels of thought common to
every human being? Define them in your own words.

1.

_____

_____

_____

_____

_____

_____

_____

_____

_____

2.

_____

_____

_____

_____

_____

_____

_____

_____

_____

Universal Thought is also known as Infinite Intelligence.
What does access to Infinite Intelligence bring to your
endeavors, your relationships, and your life experience?

_____

_____

_____

_____

_____

Which mode of thinking helps us maintain a lighthearted perspective? How?

_____

_____

_____

_____

_____

_____

_____

_____

_____

_____

The analytical channel of thought is entirely based in the past and is made up of memory. What are some characteristics of this mode of thought?

_____

_____

_____

_____

_____

_____

_____

_____

_____

Too much analytical thinking can result in exhaustion.
Discuss how this is true.

_____

_____

_____

_____

_____

_____

_____

_____

_____

How is analytical or process thinking useful and
even essential?

_____

_____

_____

_____

_____

_____

_____

_____

_____

"Flow" thought is available when we are present and in
the moment. What does being present in the moment make
available to you and your world?

_____

_____

_____

_____

_____
_____
_____
_____
_____
_____
_____

Solutions and insights emerge from being present in the Now.
How does this make sense to you?

_____
_____
_____
_____
_____
_____
_____
_____
_____
_____

Feelings that arise from analytical thinking are always
contingent on something _____ . How is it helpful
to realize this?

_____
_____
_____
_____
_____
_____
_____
_____
_____
_____

Identify some experiential and perceptual benefits that
originate from the higher-order feelings of Flow.

_____

_____

_____

_____

_____

_____

_____

_____

_____

_____

What becomes available to you once you distinguish the
analytical channel of thinking?

_____

_____

_____

_____

_____

_____

_____

_____

_____

_____

What is meant by "impersonal" thought? What is available to
you when you can distinguish this mode of thought?

_____

_____

_____

_____

_____

Which mode of thinking recognizes that you are caught up in your thinking? What becomes available to you once you recognize this? Explain.

Give an example in your life when you have been in the diffuse thinking of Flow. How did it feel? What were you able to accomplish?

CHAPTER 4

Transformational Humor

Positive Transformational Change

*Flow with whatever may happen
and let your mind be free.
Stay centered by accepting
whatever you are doing.
This is the ultimate.*

—CHUANG TZU

In your own words, describe "Transformational Humor."

_____

_____

_____

_____

_____

What is meant by a "humor continuum"?

Once realized, how would taking your perceptual cues from the realm of Transformational Humor impact your everyday life?

Do you have a personal experience or story in which you were coming from Transformational Humor? If so, what was it and what difference did it make for you?

_____

_____

_____

_____

_____

_____

_____

_____

_____

_____

_____

_____

_____

_____

What are three positive ways of being that one may access from alignment with Transformational Humor?

_____

_____

_____

_____

_____

_____

_____

_____

_____

_____

_____

_____

_____

A transformational shift would be one in which there is a fundamental shift in perception. In what area or areas of your life would you like to have a transformational shift?

_____

_____

_____

_____

_____

_____

_____

_____

_____

_____

_____

_____

How could you make such transformational shifts?

_____

_____

_____

_____

_____

_____

_____

_____

_____

_____

_____

_____

CHAPTER 5

Purpose

A path is made by walking on it.

—CHUANG TZU

In general, we tend to take our cues about how we're doing from either internal or external input. Distinguish for yourself benefits and drawbacks from both frames of reference.

Our external experience is reflective of our what?

How does personal thought create your personal experience?

Form manifests as a result of the Universal Law of Thought. What do you see now that you didn't see before reflecting on this law?

_____
_____
_____
_____
_____
_____
_____

Who you authentically are inspires your personal purpose.
What inspires you?

_____
_____
_____
_____
_____
_____
_____
_____
_____

In terms of "personal purpose," what is the vision you have
for expressing your most authentic self?

_____
_____
_____
_____
_____
_____
_____
_____
_____

What is at least one example of an invalidating internal conversation that you have personally experienced?

_____

_____

_____

_____

_____

_____

_____

_____

_____

_____

_____

_____

Listening to your invalidating conversations keeps you from realizing your full self-expression. What are some specific repercussions of listening to your internal invalidating conversations?

_____

_____

_____

_____

_____

_____

_____

_____

_____

_____

_____

_____

As best you can, from the present moment of creative flow thinking—meaning paying no attention to thinking from the past—write a statement that captures who you see yourself to be when inspired and authentically self-expressed.

Jump in! Start with what inspires you now. This statement will likely evolve and change over time, as you grow into its expression and eventually outgrow it into more expansive and expressive words.

CHAPTER 6

The Silence

There are no others.

—RAMANA MAHARSHI

All healing transmutation takes place in the Silence. Find an example from your own life to illustrate this.

_____

_____

_____

_____

_____

_____

_____

_____

_____

_____

_____
_____
_____
_____

Authentic elevation of mood is a direct indicator of elevation
of the quality of thought. Can you think of a time when you
were struggling over a condition or circumstance, and a shift
in mood allowed for a lightening of the struggle—allowed for
a lighter perspective on the circumstance to emerge? Think
of at least one example from your own life experience that
demonstrates this.

_____
_____
_____
_____
_____
_____
_____
_____
_____
_____
_____
_____

Is a skeptical approach a healthy approach? Why or why not?

_____
_____
_____
_____
_____
_____

_____
_____
_____
_____
_____
_____
_____

What is meant by the statement: "The questions themselves are the precursors to the answers"?

_____
_____
_____
_____
_____
_____
_____
_____
_____
_____
_____

What is one benefit of developing a deeper alignment with the Silence?

_____
_____
_____
_____
_____
_____

Silence is the realm of Infinite Intelligence. What does this mean?

Your vibrational alignment with the Silence resonates and can catalyze an awakening in another person. Please elaborate on how this occurs. What are some of the possible effects of such a transference?

_____

_____

_____

_____

_____

_____

What is an indication of how alignment with Silence appears
or occurs within you? What is an example?

_____

_____

_____

_____

_____

_____

_____

_____

_____

_____

_____

_____

There is a way of being that generates no resistance. What is
it? What is it indicative of, and what is its value?

_____

_____

_____

_____

_____

_____

_____

_____

How is creative genius available to each and every human being? Please elaborate.

A "change agent" is a person who has cultivated the capacity to deal with their own inner turmoil, frustrations, and inauthentic expressions of self. In what ways are you being a change agent?

What constitutes a "natural change agent"?

_____

_____

_____

_____

_____

_____

_____

_____

_____

_____

_____

How and where have you been a change agent in your life?

_____

_____

_____

_____

_____

_____

_____

_____

_____

_____

_____

How is personal freedom generated?

What is the outcome of taking your cues from the external environment? What is the outcome of taking your cues from the internal compass? Could both be valuable? If so, in what ways?

_____

_____

_____

_____

_____

_____

Your responses to tragedy or traumatic experiences originate
in _____ .

_____

_____

_____

_____

_____

_____

_____

_____

_____

_____

_____

_____

The self-realized person is living from alignment with
the Silence, the realm of Infinite Intelligence, Omniscient
Wisdom, and Omnipotent Love. How could you develop
yourself to align with the Silence and cause positive change?

_____

_____

_____

_____

CHAPTER 7

Being

There is no way home.
Home is the Way.

—THICH NHAT HANH

An inward outlook is a state of mind that serves as a conduit for positive, effortless change. In developing an inward outlook, where could you be of most service?

_____

_____

_____

_____

_____

_____

_____

_____
_____
_____
_____
_____
_____

What could compassionate humor mean to you in your
daily life?

_____
_____
_____
_____
_____
_____
_____
_____
_____
_____

"Being catalyzes Being." Please elaborate on this in your
own words.

_____
_____
_____
_____
_____
_____

Identify at least two benefits for others that emerge from practicing listening from curiosity and authentic interest, being present in the moment, with nothing from your personal past on your mind.

"Bring what you are looking for." What does this statement mean to you? Is it an empowering statement? If so, how?

_____
_____
_____
_____
_____
_____

The Inward Outlook is the expressed attitude of
Transformational Humor. It is a way of Being. What do
you now see about living from an inward outlook that you
did not see before reading this book?

_____
_____
_____
_____
_____
_____
_____
_____
_____
_____
_____

AFTERWORD

I AM FILLED WITH GRATITUDE FOR THE PEOPLE with whom I have had the great good fortune to work. I have a deep appreciation for the attitude of service and humility that characterizes all those who choose to deal with their own inauthenticity and reactivity in order to learn, respond, and live from this transformative paradigm. Interaction with them has revealed to me the extent to which people experience positive empowering perceptual shifts and resultant outward action in their life and work when they rely on an inward outlook.

What also demonstrates to be true is that, even with those of us for whom lightheartedness is key, ongoing inquiry into living from this inward outlook has us reevaluate the depth and richness available through being present in the moment. Such reflection augments the power of what we are already doing and expands it into a heightened awareness of what positive transformational change is possible.

As human beings, we are conscious or unconscious masters in our own worlds. We either consciously or unconsciously choose and create our experiences of reality through personal thought. Understanding the principles underlying *The Inward*

Outlook, we have the advantage of *consciously* choosing which thinking we pay attention to. We thus masterfully, *consciously*, create our experience in the world, noncontingent on outer circumstances.

The possibility of integrating this understanding is that it will inspire you to rely more and more on an inward outlook as the expression of your way of being in the world. This way of being facilitates personal change and brings the ease and power of living in the present moment.

Then, as we expand our inner awareness outward toward the realization of peace, well-being, and joy for family, community, and the world, we usher in the evolution of what's possible for human beings.

ACKNOWLEDGMENTS

WITH MUCH GRATITUDE FOR THE ENLIGHTENED teachings of the Reverend Kathryn Jarvis and the work of Mr. Sydney Banks, from which the inspiration for this book was ignited.

Many thanks to my extraordinary clients. I am grateful to have had time with you over the years, and I admire all of you for your commitment to distinguish who you are authentically, expanding your contribution to the world.

My deepest gratitude to the many mentors I have had, who have shared not only their teachings but also their wisdom through how they live and lived their lives. It is my hope that this book lays a few more foundational bricks in the evolving evolutionary path toward awakening.

With many thanks to my creative and aesthetically astute associate, Mary Ann Casler. Without her invaluable creativity and support, this redesigned book would not have been brought to fruition.

And to my dear family, friends, and colleagues, who lent their support through the less hopeful moments, I am ever grateful.

In this sense, the writing of this book was a group effort.

GLOSSARY

Awaken: By "awaken," I mean, quite literally, to wake up from one's perceived current reality. An awakening is a shift in consciousness that moves us from the world of form into the previously unrealized oneness with Universal Truth. Awakening is often experienced as a process, although it can occur as a sudden or dramatic new state.

Core Values: Core values are values that, for any given human being or culture, are irreducible to what is most basically meaningful in life experience. They are values that are both personally and culturally essential, for their ballast is intrinsic, not contingent on outer circumstances or conditions. Conscious connection to your core values gives conscious access to your purpose, which is the compass to your authentic expression of yourself, your "true north."

Lightheartedness: Lightheartedness is a calm feeling of confidence and a certainty of hopefulness, no matter what the circumstance or condition. It emerges as we realize that the source of our experience is our personal thinking. Consequently, we choose to turn our attention away from personal thought and listen from the Silence, which emanates possibility and Joy.

Paradigm: By "paradigm," I am referring to a distinct set of concepts within a framework that focuses on a particular understanding of the nature of being. Regarding *The Inward Outlook* paradigm, its discipline and methodology are practiced toward actualizing self-realization—an awakening to one's authentic self.

Positive Transformational Change: Positive transformational change refers to a movement in the direction of an individual's, organization's, or community's purpose and vision, which are based on core values. The accomplishment of these commitments in healthy, lighthearted, creative, and respectful ways takes place as a result of a shift in perspective—in other words, within a context of transformational humor. Accomplishment of authentically expressed purpose aligned with vision constitutes positive transformational change.

Transformational Humor: "Transformational humor" is a term I am using to describe a perceptual vantage point toward life in general that is quietly contented and hopeful. It is a perspective permeated with a deep and unflappable sense of knowing that in spite of all appearances to the contrary, there is hopefulness and an inherent order that moves toward a positive good. This knowing becomes the catalyst for hopefulness not only in yourself but in others, thus propelling all toward positive change. This state of mind sees the best in each individual, organization, situation, and circumstance.

Transformational humor delightfully anticipates the unexpected and at the same time allows for the foibles of humanity without judgment. The developed capacity for this type of perception also embodies the experience and expression of the attributes of Joy and Compassion, nomenclature I occasionally use interchangeably with transformational humor. These terms reference access to Divine Attributes of the Formless, the Source of All That Is.

Transformational Impact: Transformational impact refers to a significant influence that catalyzes a restructuring of perception, which can then result in a variety of previously unseen alternative choices. It is a step-change that shifts the status quo.

ABOUT THE AUTHOR

LAURA BASHA, PHD, is a published author, professional artist, certified trainer, public speaker, and organizational psychologist. She holds a BA in fine arts, an MA in counseling psychology, and a combined doctorate in clinical and organizational psychology.

Through the years, the focus of her work has always been personal and organizational transformation and leadership development, as well as creativity, beauty, and spirituality. She has been an international consultant, educator, and personal coach for thousands of clients since 1978.

Dr. Basha resides in Northern California with her husband and their beloved Tibetan Terrier, Bodhi.

You can view her work on her website:
www.whitebirdrising.com

Author photo © Reenie Raschke

SELECTED TITLES FROM SHE WRITES PRESS

She Writes Press is an independent publishing company founded to serve women writers everywhere. Visit us at www.shewritespress.com.

Think Better. Live Better. 5 Steps to Create the Life You Deserve by Francine Huss. $16.95, 978-1-938314-66-7. With the help of this guide, readers will learn to cultivate more creative thoughts, realign their mindset, and gain a new perspective on life.

Rethinking Possible: A Memoir of Resilience by Rebecca Faye Smith Galli. $16.95, 978-1-63152-220-8. After her brother's devastatingly young death tears her world apart, Becky Galli embarks upon a quest to recreate the sense of family she's lost—and learns about healing and the transformational power of love over loss along the way.

This Way Up: Seven Tools for Unleashing Your Creative Self and Transforming Your Life by Patti Clark. $16.95, 978-1-63152-028-0. A story of healing for women who yearn to lead a fuller life, accompanied by a workbook designed to help readers work through personal challenges, discover new inspiration, and harness their creative power.

Negatively Ever After: A Skeptic's Guide to Finding Happiness by Deanna K. Willmon. $16.95, 978-1-63152-312-0. From achieving self-adoration and learning what gratitude truly means to determining whether sharing happiness is really a good idea, this realistic and accessible guide will help you harness your negativity and find your own inner happiness.

Brave(ish): A Memoir of a Recovering Perfectionist by Margaret Davis Ghielmetti. $16.95, 978-1-63152-747-0. An intrepid traveler sets off at forty to live the expatriate dream overseas—only to discover that she has no idea how to live even her own life. Part travelogue and part transformation tale, Ghielmetti's memoir, narrated with humor and warmth, proves that it's never too late to reconnect with our authentic selves—if we dare to put our own lives first at last.

Note to Self: A Seven-Step Path to Gratitude and Growth by Laurie Buchanan. $16.95, 978-1-63152-113-3. Transforming intention into action, *Note to Self* equips you to shed your baggage, bridging the gap between where you are and where you want to be—body, mind, and spirit—and empowering you to step into joy-filled living *now!*